THE AMERICAN PEOPLE

- *The Native American People of the East*
- *The Native American People of the West*
- *The American People in Colonial New England*
- *The American People in the Colonial South*
- *The American People in the Antebellum North*
- *The American People in the Antebellum South*
- *The American People on the Western Frontier*
- *The American People in the Industrial City*
- *The American People in the Depression*
- *The American People in the Age of Kennedy*

The Native American People Of the East

Edited by
JAMES AXTELL

ℙ

Pendulum Press, Inc. West Haven, Connecticut

Clothbound Edition ISBN 0-88301-082-8 Complete Set
0-88301-083-6 This Volume

Paperback Edition   ISBN 0-88301-066-6 Complete Set
0-88301-067-4 This Volume

Library of Congress Catalog Card Number 72-95875

Published by
Pendulum Press, Inc.
The Academic Building
Saw Mill Road
West Haven, Connecticut 06516

Printed in the United States of America

Cover Design by Dick Brassil, Silverman Design Group

CONTENTS

ABOUT THE EDITOR

James Axtell, the recipient of a B.A. degree from Yale University and a Ph.D. from Cambridge University, has also studied at Oxford University and was a postdoctoral fellow at Harvard University. Mr. Axtell has taught history at Yale and is currently Associate Professor of Anglo-American History at Sarah Lawrence College. He is on the editorial board of *History of Education Quarterly* and has been a consultant to the American Council of Learned Societies. He has published several articles and reviews and is the author of a forthcoming book, *The School upon a Hill: Education and Society in Colonial New England.*

FOREWORD

The American People is founded on the belief that the study of history in the schools and junior levels of college generally begins at the wrong end. It usually begins with abstract and pre-digested *conclusions*—the conclusions of other historians as filtered through the pen of a textbook writer—and not with the primary sources of the past and unanswered *questions*—the starting place of the historian himself.

Since we all need, use, and think about the past in our daily lives, we are all historians. The question is whether we can be skillful, accurate, and useful historians. The only way to become such. is to exercise our historical skills and interests until we gain competence. But we have to exercise them in the same ways the best historians do or we will be kidding ourselves that we are *doing* history when in fact we are only absorbing sponge-like the results of someone else's historical competence.

Historical competence must begin with one crucial skill—the ability to distinguish between past and present. Without a sharp sense of the past as a different time from our own, we will be unable to accord the people of the past the respect that we would like to receive from the people of the future. And without according them that respect, we will be unable to recognize their integrity as individuals or to understand them as human beings.

A good sense of the past depends primarily on a good sense of the present, on experience, and on the imaginative empathy to relate ourselves to human situations not our own. Although most students have had a relatively brief experience of life and have not yet given full expression to their imaginative sympathies, they do possess the one essential prerequisite for the study of history—the lives they have lived from birth to young adulthood. This should be the initial focus of their study of the past, not remotely adult experiences to which they cannot yet relate, such as politics, diplomacy, and war.

Thus the organizing perspective of this series is the universal life experiences that all people have: being born, growing up, loving and marrying, working and playing, behaving and misbehaving, worshipping, and dying. As only he could, Shakespeare portrayed these cycles in *As You Like It* (Act II, scene vii):

> All the world's a stage,
> And all the men and women merely players.
> They have their exits and their entrances;
> And one man in his time plays many parts,
> His acts being seven ages. At first the infant,
> Mewling and puking in the nurse's arms.
> And then the whining school-boy, with his satchel
> And shining morning face, creeping like snail
> Unwillingly to school. And then the lover,
> Sighing like furnace, with a woeful ballad
> Made to his mistress' eyebrow. Then a soldier,
> Full of strange oaths, and bearded like a pard;
> Jealous in honour, sudden and quick in quarrel,
> Seeking the bubble reputation
> Even in the cannon's mouth. And then the justice,
> In fair round belly with good capon lined,
> With eyes severe and beard of formal cut,
> Full of wise saws and modern instances;
> And so he plays his part. The sixth age shifts
> Into the lean and slipper'd pantaloon,
> With spectacles on nose and pouch on side;
> His youthful hose, well saved, a world too wide
> For his shrunk shank; and his big manly voice,
> Turning again toward childish treble, pipes
> And whistles in his sound. Last scene of all,
> That ends this strange eventful history,
> Is second childishness, and mere oblivion,
> Sans teeth, sans eyes, sans taste, sans everything.

These are experiences to which any student can relate and from which he can learn, simply because they surround him daily in his home, community, and not least, school.

There is an additional reason for focussing on the universal life cycle. If history is everything that happened in the past, obviously some things were and are more important than others. Until fairly recently the things historians have found important have been the turning points or *changes* in history—"great" men and "great" events. But recently, with the help of anthropologists, historians have come to a greater awareness of the importance of stability and inertia, of *non-*change in society. For every society—and therefore its history—is a mixture of change and stability, of generally long periods of fixity punctuated now and then by moments of modification and change.

The major reason for the stability of society is the conservative bent of human behavior and ideals, the desire to preserve, hold, fix, and keep stable. People acquire habits and habits impede change. The habits people acquire are the common ways the members of a society react to the world—how they behave and feel and think in common—which distinguish them from other societies and cultures. So at bottom history is about ordinary people, how they did things alike and together that gave continuity and durability to their society so that it could change to meet new circumstances without completely losing its former identity and character.

America is such a society and *The American People* is an attempt to provide representative selections from primary sources about the lives and habits of ordinary people in periods of history that are usually known in textbooks for their great changes.

Since the experience of each student is the only prerequisite for the study of primary sources at the first level, annotations and introductory material have been reduced to a minimum, simply enough to identify the sources, their authors, and the circumstances in which they were written.

But the remains of the past are mute by themselves. Many sources have survived that can tell us what happened in the past and why, but they have to be questioned properly to reveal their secrets. So by way of illustration, a number of questions have been asked in each chapter, but these should be supplemented by the students whose experiences and knowledge and interests are, after all, the flywheel of the educational process. Although the questions and sources are divided into chapters, they should be used freely in the other chapters; the collection should be treated as a whole. And although most of the illustrative questions are confined to the sources at hand, questions that extend to the present should be asked to anchor the acquired knowledge of the past in the immediate experience of the present. Only then will learning be real and lasting and history brought to life.

INTRODUCTION:

When Columbus sailed into the coastal waters of America, the first thing he discovered was not a naked continent but a bevy of "naked people" to whom he gave "some red caps and some glass beads." And unlike the steady stream of missionaries, traders, and colonists who followed in their wake, Columbus and his fellow explorers of the Atlantic coast were the only Europeans to observe the native American people in something like their natural state. For as soon as Europeans landed and began to impose their different ways of life upon the natives—even the name *"Indians"* is a European invention based on a serious case of mistaken identity—the cultures of America intersected with the cultures of Europe.

This is a fact of great importance for anyone interested in the history of the American Indian way of life. It means, on the one hand, that the first written accounts of the Indians came from the pens of white men, from European travellers who encountered the Indians on their sightseeing tours of the New World. Fortunately, for their descendents who are interested in Indian culture, they were fascinated by the novelty of Indian life and so were led to make detailed commentaries on the everyday lives of the people. It also means that the writer's purpose in coming to America, the particular time at which he did so, and his own cultural background inevitably colored his view of the Indians, though in ways that are not always predictable. Did the missionaries, for example, always think that the Indians were the devil's disciples? Did the traders always suspect that their Indian customers were out to cheat them? Did the white captives always see their captors as blood-thirsty savages? The historical accounts by no means agree, and our task, as historians, is to put away our stereotypes of both Indians and whites and to find out why.

In so doing, we should ask several guiding questions: In what ways does the observer's European background affect the *objectivity* of his views of the Indians? Does it negate *all* value they might have as historical testimony? Is there any such thing as complete objectivity in people's descriptions and judgments of other people? Should the effort to be objective even be made? Does the historian, like a judge or a jury, owe justice to the people he is describing? What role, then, does objectivity play in the search for justice?

The subjects of the Europeans' curiosity were the Indian tribes that belonged to the Algonkin and Iroquoian language groups. Geographically, they extended from the Massachusetts and Delawares on the Atlantic coast north to the Micmacs, Algonquins, and Hurons of lower Canada and the St. Lawrence River, south to the Tuscororas, Cherokees, and Powhatans of Virginia and the Carolinas, and west as far as the Ojibwas and Winnebagos of Minnesota and the Great Lakes. What their ways of life were like when the Europeans "discovered" them is the subject of the following chapters.

I. BIRTH

According to Shakespeare, a sixteenth-century English baby would most likely be found ". . . . mewling and puking in the nurse's arms." Were Indian babies entrusted to wet-nurses? What was the physical condition of Indian mothers after giving birth? Did they have a long lying-in period—as much as a month—like English women? Were Indian babies likely to be "mewling and puking" after birth? How were their physical needs cared for? their emotional needs? How were they treated to prepare them for Indian life? From their written accounts, what can you tell about how the Europeans reacted to this treatment? Were they incredulous? shocked? admiring?

Gabriel Sagard was a French-born lay brother of the Recollects, a branch of the Franciscan order of the Catholic Church. He came to Canada in June 1623, to minister to the Hurons and returned to France a year later. From his experience he wrote The Long Journey to the Country of the Hurons *(Paris, 1632), which has been translated by H.H. Langston and edited by George M. Wrong for* The Champlain Society Publications, *volume 25 (1939). The following excerpt appears on pp. 127-131.*

In spite of the women giving themselves free play with others than their husbands and the husbands with others than their wives, it is a fact that they all are very fond of their children, in obedience to that law of caring for them which Nature has implanted in the hearts of all animals. Now what makes them love their children, however vicious and wanting in respect, more than is the case here is that they are the support of their parents in old age, either helping them to a living or else defending them from their enemies, and Nature preserves unimpaired its authority over them in this respect. Wherefore what they most desire is to have many children, to be so much the stronger and assured of support in the time of their old age. And yet the women are not so prolific as they are here, perhaps as much on account of their lubricity as from choosing so many men.

When the woman bears a child the custom of the country [of the Hurons] is that she pierces the ears of the child with an awl or a fishbone and puts in the quill of a feather or something else to keep the hole open, and afterwards suspends to it wampum beads or other trifles, and also hangs them round the child's neck however small it may be. There are some also who even make them swallow grease or oil as soon as they are born; I do not know the purpose or reason, unless it is that the devil, who apes the work of God, has chosen to devise and impose upon them this practice, in order to mimic in certain respects holy baptism or some other sacrament of the Church.

In giving names they follow tradition, that is to say they have a great supply of names from which they choose in order to bestow them on their children. Some names have no meaning; others have, such as *Yocoisse*, the wind, *Ongyata*, the neck, *Tochingo*, crane, *Sondaqua*, eagle, *Scouta*, the head, *Tonra*, the belly, *Taihy*, a tree, etc. I saw one man who was called Joseph, but I was not able to learn who had given him that name, and perhaps among such a number of names as they have there may be found some resembling our own.

The ancient German women were praised by Tacitus because each fed her children at her own breast and would have been unwilling that any other than herself should give them milk. Our savage women also nourish their children with milk from their own breasts, and since they do not know the use or suitability of pap they give them the very same meat that they take themselves, after chewing it well, and so by degrees they bring them up. If the mother happens to die before the child is weaned the father takes water in which Indian corn has been thoroughly boiled and fills his mouth with it, then putting the child's mouth against his own makes it take and swallow the liquid, and this is to make up for the lack of the breast and of pap; just so I saw it done by the husband of the woman savage whom we baptized. The women use the same method in feeding the puppies of their bitches, but I found this very displeasing and nasty, to put their mouth in this way to the puppies' muzzles, which are often not too clean.

During the day they swathe their children upon a little wooden board, on which sometimes there is a rest or small bit of wood bent into a semi-circle under the feet, and they stand it up on the floor of the lodge, unless they carry the child with them when they go out, with this board on their back fastened to a belt, which is supported on the forehead; or they take them out of their swaddling clothes and carry them wrapped up in their dress above the girdle in front, or behind their back almost straight up, the child's head outside, looking from side to side over the shoulders of the woman who carries it.

When the child is swaddled on this board, which is usually decked out with little paintings and strings of wampum beads, they leave an opening in front of its private parts through which it makes water, and if the child is a girl they arrange a leaf of Indian corn upside down which serves to carry the water outside without the child being soiled with its water; and instead of napkins, for they have none, they put under it the beautifully soft down of a kind of reed on which it lies quite comfortably, and they clean it with the same down. At night they put it to bed quite naked between the father and the mother, without any accident happening, or very seldom. In other tribes I have seen them, in order to put the child to sleep, lay it in its wrappings on a skin which is hung up, tied by the four corners to the wooden supports and poles of the lodge, like the reed hammocks of sailors under the ship's deck, and when they want to rock the child they have only from time to time to give a push to the skin thus suspended.

The Cimbri used to put their new-born children into the snow to harden them to suffering, and our savages do no less; for not only do they leave them naked in the lodge, but the children, even when rather big, roll, run about, and play in the snow and during the greatest heat of summer [naked], without receiving any harm, as I have seen in many instances, wondering that these tender little bodies could endure such great cold and such great heat, according to the weather and the season, without being disordered by them. And hence it is that they become so inured to pain and toil that when they have grown up and are old and white-haired they remain always strong and vigorous, and feel hardly any discomfort or indisposition. Even the women with child are so strong that they give birth by themselves, and for the most part do not lie up. I have seen some of them come in from the woods, laden with a big bundle of wood, and give birth to a child as soon as they arrive; then immediately they are on their feet at their ordinary employment.

Since the children of such marriages cannot be vouched for as legitimate, this custom prevails among them, as well as in many other parts of the West Indies, that the children do not succeed to their father's property; but the fathers constitute the children of their own sisters their successors and heirs, since they are sure that these are of their blood and parentage. Nevertheless they love their children dearly, in spite of the doubt that they are really their own, and of the fact that they are for the most part very naughty children, paying them little respect, and hardly more obedience; for unhappily in these lands the young have no respect for the old, nor are children obedient to their parents, and moreover there is no punishment for any fault. For this reason everybody lives in complete freedom and does what he thinks fit; and parents, for failure to punish their children, are often compelled to suffer wrong-doing at their hands, sometimes being beaten and flouted to their face. This is conduct too shocking and smacks of nothing less than the brute beast. Bad example, and bad bringing up, without punishment or correction, are the causes of all this lack of decency.

Chrestien Le Clercq was a French Recollect priest who came to Canada in 1675 to minister to the Indians who occupied the rocky coasts of the Gulf of St. Lawrence from Gaspé to Cape Breton. After labors of twelve years he returned to France where his New Relations of Gaspesia *was published in 1691. It was edited and translated by William F. Ganong for* The Champlain Society Publications, *volume 5 (1910), where the following excerpt appears on pp. 88-92.*

It is not with our Gaspesians as with the Cimbrians, who plunged their children into the snow in order to harden them to the cold and to accustom them to fatigue, nor as with some of our ancient Gauls, who threw them into the water as soon as they were born, in the

belief that those which floated and came to the surface in their strug-
gles were truly legitimate, while those which sank to the bottom were
to be considered as bastards and illegitimate. The Indians wash their
children in the river as soon as they are born, and then they make
them swallow some bear's, or seal, oil. In place of a cradle, they
make the children rest upon a little board, which they cover with
skins of beaver, or with some other furs. The women adorn this little
cradle carefully with certain bits of bead-work, with wampum, porcupine quills, and certain figures which they form with their paints.
This is in order to beautify it, and to render it just so much the finer
in proportion as they love their children. For these they make little
garments of skins, which are all painted and adorned with the pret-
tiest and most curious things they possess. They are accouched with
very great ease, and carry very heavy burdens during their pregnancy. Some indeed, finding themselves overtaken by this illness in going
to fetch wood, retire a little apart in order to bring the child into the
world; and they carry the wood to the wigwam upon their backs, with
the new born babe in their arms, as if nothing at all had happened.
An Indian woman, when in a canoe one day, feeling herself pressed
by the pains of childbirth, asked those of her company to put her on
shore, and to wait for her a moment. She entered alone into the
woods, where she was delivered of a boy; she brought him to the canoe, which she helped to paddle all the rest of the journey. They
never give birth to a child in the wigwam, for the men never give it up
to them. The men remain therein whilst the wife is delivered in the
woods at the foot of a tree. If she suffers pains, her arms are attached
above to some pole, her nose, ears, and mouth being stopped up. After this she is pressed strongly on the sides, in order to force the child
to issue from the belly of its mother. If she feels it a little too
severely, she calls on the jugglers, who come with joy, in order to ex-
tort some smoking tobacco, or other things of which they have need.
They say that this is a present which they ask for their Ouahiche, that
is to say, their demon, in order that he may chase and remove the
germ which hinders the accouchement . . .

Our Gaspesians are not so ridiculous as the Indians of South
America, who at the same moment that their wives are accouched,
betake themselves to bed, as if they had themselves suffered the pains
and the cramps of childbirth, whilst their wives, with all their

relatives and their friends, endeavour to console this imaginary invalid, to whom they give a thousand kindnesses and the best of everything that they have. The Indians have too much spirit to be willing to pass for women newly accouched, although they comfort their consorts with much charity. They go hunting for the purpose of providing the wherewithal for supporting their wives, in order that these may suckle their babes. For it is a thing unheard of, that they should give them out to be nursed, since they cannot persuade themselves to yield to others the fruits of their own bowels. By this conduct they reproach the lack of feeling of those mothers who abandon these little innocents to the care of nurses, from whom very often they suck corruption with the milk. That this is true has been illustrated by unhappy experience in the conduct of Alexander the Great, and of the Emperor Caligula. The first of these, according to Saint Clement of Alexandria, used to get drunk as a beast, because his mother was subject to wine. The second, according to the testimony of history, breathed only blood and carnage, even to a point where he passionately wished that the Roman people had but a single head, in order that he might be able by a single blow to decapitate all the citizens of that powerful Republic; and this was because his nurse, in order to accustom him to cruelty, and to inspire in him a savage disposition, reddened with her blood the ends of her nipples. Our poor Indian women have so much affection for their children that they do not rate the quality of nurse any lower than that of mother. They even suckle the children up to the age of four or five years, and, when these begin to eat, the mothers chew the meat in order to induce the children to swallow it. One cannot express the tenderness and affection which the fathers and mothers have for their children. I have seen considerable presents offered to the parents in order that these might give the children to certain Frenchmen who would have taken them to France. But this would have torn their hearts, and millions would not induce them to abandon their children for a moment.

Adriaen Van der Donck, a law graduate of the University of Leyden, came to the New Netherlands in 1641 as the resident legal officer for the large Van Rensselaer patroonship along the Hudson

River. In 1649, he returned to Holland to protest Peter Stuyvesant's mismanagement of the colony. Five years of bureaucratic red tape enabled him to write his Description of the New Netherlands *(1655). The first English translation was made in 1841 by Jeremiah Johnson and published in the* Collections of the New-York Historical Society, *2nd series, volume 1. The following excerpt is taken from Thomas F. O'Donnell's reprint of that translation (Syracuse, 1968), pp. 84-86.*

Whenever a native female is pregnant, in wedlock or otherwise, they take care that they do no act that would injure the offspring. During pregnancy they are generally healthy, and they experience little or no sickness or painful days, and when the time of their delivery is near (which they calculate closely), and they fear a severe accouchement, or if it be their first time, then they prepare a drink made of a decoction of roots that grow in the woods, which are known by them, and they depart alone to a secluded place near a brook, or stream of water, where they can be protected from the winds, and prepare a shelter for themselves with mats and covering, where, provided with provisions necessary for them, they await their delivery without the company or aid of any person. After their children are born, and if they are males, although the weather be ever so cold and freezing, they immerse them some time in the water, which, they say, makes them strong brave men and hardy hunters. After the immersion they wrap their children in warm clothing and pay them great attention from fear of accidents, and after they have remained several days in their secluded places, again return to their homes and friends. They rarely are sick from childbirth, suffer no inconveniences upon the same, nor do any of them die on such occasions. Upon this subject some persons assign, as a reason and cause for their extraordinary deliveries, that the knowledge of good and evil is not given to them, as unto us; that therefore they do not suffer the pains of sin in bringing forth their children; that such pains are really not natural, but the punishment which follows the knowledge of sin, as committed by our first mother, and is attached to those only; others ascribe the cause of the difference to the salubrity of the climate, their well-formed bodies, and their manner of living.

The native Indian women of every grade always nurse their own children, nor do we know of any who have trusted that parental duty to others. About New Amsterdam, and for many miles and days' journey into the interior, I have never heard of but a few instances of native women, who did not take good care of their children, or who trusted them to the nursing and care of others; when they suckle or are pregnant, they in those cases practice the strictest abstinence, because, as they say, it is beneficial to their offspring, and to nursing children. In the meantime, their women are not precise or offended, if their husbands have foreign associations, but they observe the former custom so religiously, that they hold it to be disgraceful for a woman to recede from it before her child is weaned, which they usually do when their children are a year old, and those who wean their children before that period are despised. During a certain season, their women seclude themselves, and do not appear abroad or permit themselves to be seen of men; if they are at one of their great feasts or public assemblies, and the fountain springs, they retire immediately if possible, and do not appear abroad again until the season is over. Otherwise when all is well, and they are not betrothed, they frequently are light of behaviour, as well the women as the men, and yield to temptation without shame; but foul and impertinent language, which is common with the lower class with us, is despised with them. All romping, caressing, and wanton behaviour they speak of with contempt, and say that they are indirect allurements to unchastity. If they observe such behaviour among the Netherlanders, they reprove the parties, and bid them seek retirement. What better reproof can be given to such levity? Some of their chiefs and great men have two or three wives, who will readily accommodate a visiting friend with one of his women for a night; but if it takes place without his consent, the act is deemed a disgrace, and the woman is chastised and sent away.

Robert Beverley (1673-1722) was the second son of a wealthy Virginia planter. After an English education he began a short career in Virginia government which ended in 1705 when he returned to England to argue a land case before the Privy Council. There he published The History and Present State of Virginia *(1705), which has been reprinted by Louis B. Wright (1947) and David Freeman Hawke (1971). The following passage comes from pp. 92-93 of Hawke's edition.*

The manner of the Indians treating their young children is very strange, for instead of keeping them warm at their first entry into the world and wrapping them up with I don't know how many cloths, according to our fond custom, the first thing they do is to dip the child over head and ears in cold water and then to bind it naked to a convenient board, having a hole fitly placed for evacuation; but they always put cotton, wool, fur, or other soft thing for the body to rest easy on between the child and the board. In this posture they keep it several months, till the bones begin to harden, the joints to knit, and the limbs to grow strong; and then they let it loose from the board, suffering it to crawl about, except when they are feeding or playing with it.

While the child is thus at the board, they either lay it flat on its back or set it leaning on one end, or else hang it up by a string fastened to the upper end of the board for that purpose, the child and board being all this while carried about together. As our women undress their children to clean them and shift their linen, so they do theirs to wash and grease them.

The method the women have of carrying their children after they are suffered to crawl about is very particular: they carry them at their backs in summer, taking one leg of the child under their arm and the counter arm of the child in their hand over their shoulder, the other leg hanging down, and the child all the while holding fast with its other hand, but in winter they carry them in the hollow of their matchcoat at their back, leaving nothing but the child's head out.

John Lawson, a well-educated English gentleman, came to North Carolina in 1700, where he helped to found Bath Town, the colony's first town. Active in encouraging colonization and in surveying for eight years, he returned to London in 1709 to attend the publication of A New Voyage to Carolina *which appeared in that year. He was killed by the Tuscorora Indians in 1711 on an exploration of the Neuse River. The following passage is taken from the reprint of 1937 published in Richmond, Virginia, pp. 200-201.*

The Savage Women of America have very easy Travail with their Children; sometimes they bring Twins, and are brought to bed by themselves, when took at a Disadvantage; not but they have Mid-wives amongst them, as well as Doctors who make it their Profession (for Gain) to assist and deliver Women, and some of these Midwives are very knowing in several Medicines that Carolina affords, which certainly expedite, and make easy Births. Besides, they are unacquainted with those severe Pains which follow the Birth in our European Women. Their Remedies are a great Cause of this Easiness in that State; for the Indian Women will run up and down the Plantation the same day, very briskly, and without any sign of Pain or Sickness; yet they look very meagre and thin. Not but that we must allow a great deal owing to the Climate and the natural Constitution of these Women, whose Course of Nature never visits them in such Quantities, as the European Women have. And though they never want Plenty of Milk, yet I never saw an Indian Woman with very large Breasts; neither does the youngest Wife ever fail of proving so good a Nurse as to bring her Child up free from the Rickets and Disasters that proceed from the Teeth, with many other Distempers which attack our Infants in England, and other Parts of Europe. They let their Children suck till they are well grown, unless they prove big with Child sooner. They always nurse their own Children themselves, unless Sickness or Death prevents. I once saw a Nurse hired to give Suck to an Indian Woman's Child, which you have in my Journal. After Delivery, they absent the Company of a Man for forty days. As soon as the Child is born, they wash it in cold Water at the next Stream and then bedawb it, as I have mentioned before. After which the Husband takes care to provide a Cradle, which is soon made, consisting of a Piece of flat Wood, which they hew with their Hatches to the likeness of a Board; it is about two Foot long, and a Foot broad; to this they brace and tie the Child down very close, having near the middle, a Stick fastened about two Inches from the Board, which is for the Child's Breech to rest upon, under which they put a Wad of Moss that receives the Child's Excrements, by which means they can shift the moss and keep all clean and sweet. Some Nations have very flat Heads, as you have heard in my Journal, which is made whilst tied on this Cradle, as that Relation informs you. These Cradles are apt to make the Body flat; yet they are the most portable things that can be invented, for there is a String which goes from one Corner of the Board to the other, whereby the Mother flings her Child on her Back; so the Infant's Back is towards hers, and its Face looks up towards the Sky. If it rains, she throws her Leather or Woollen Match-coat, over her Head, which covers the Child all over, and secures her and it from the Injuries of rainy Weather. The Savage Women quit all Company, and dress not their own Victuals during their Purgations.

After they have had several Children, they grow strangely out of Shape in their Bodies; As for Barenness, I never knew any of their Women that have not Children when married.

John Long came to Canada from England in 1768. For twenty years he lived the strenuous life of a fur trader and served as a ranger-guide for British forces during the American Revolution. In 1788, he returned to England where his Voyages and Travels of an Indian Interpreter and Trader *was published in 1791. The following passage appears on pp. 77-80 of the edition by Milo Milton Quaife, published in Chicago in 1922.*

About an hour before sunset on the fourth day we stopped at a small creek, which was too deep to be forded, and whilst the Indian was assisting me in making a raft to cross over, rather than swim through in such cold weather against a strong current, I looked round, and missed his wife. I was rather displeased, as the sun was near setting and I was anxious to gain the opposite shore, to encamp before dark. I asked the Indian where she was gone; he smiled, and told me he supposed into the woods to set a collar for a partridge. In about an hour she returned with a newborn infant in her arms, and coming up to me, said in Chippewa, "*Oway Saggonash Payshik Shomagonish,*" or, "Here, Englishman, is a young warrior." It is said that the Indian women bring forth children with very little pain, but I believe it is merely an opinion. It is true they are strong and hardy, and will support fatigue to the moment of their delivery; but this does not prove they are exempt from the common feelings of the sex on such trying occasions. A young woman of the Rat nation has been known to be in labor a day and a night without a groan. The force of example, acting upon their pride, will not allow these poor creatures to betray a weakness or express the pain they feel, probably lest the husband should think her unworthy of his future attention, and despise both mother and child. At any rate he would tell her the infant, if a boy, would never be a warrior: and if a girl, would have a dastardly spirit, and of course neither of them be fit for a savage life.

I believe it will not be disputed that the Indian women love their children with as much affection as parents in the most civilized states can boast. Many proofs might be adduced to support this assertion. A mother suckles her child till it attains the age of four or five years, and sometimes till it is six or seven. From their infant state they endeavor to promote an independent spirit. They are never known either to beat or scold them, lest the martial disposition which is to adorn their future life and character should be weakened; on all occasions they avoid everything compulsive, that the freedom with which they wish them to think and act may not be controlled. If they die, they lament their death with unfeigned tears, and even for months after their decease will weep at the graves of their departed children. The nation of savages called *Biscatonges*, or by the French, *Pleureurs*, are said to weep more bitterly at the birth of a child than at its decease, because they look upon death only as a journey from whence he will return, but with regard to his birth, they consider it as an entrance into a life of perils and misfortunes.

As soon as a child is born, if in summer, the mother goes into the water and immerses the infant. As soon as this is done, it is wrapped up in a small blanket and tied to a flat board, covered with dry moss, in the form of the bottom of a coffin, with a hoop over the top where the head lies, to preserve it from injury. In winter it is clad in skins as well as blankets. In the heat of summer gauze is thrown over the young savage to keep off the mosquitoes, which are very troublesome in the woods. The board on which the child is placed is slung to the mother's forehead with a broad worsted belt, and rests against her back.

When the French took possession of Canada the women had neither linen nor swaddling clothes. All their child-bed furniture consisted of a kind of trough, filled with dry rotten wood dust, which is as soft as the finest down and well calculated to imbibe the moisture of the infant. On this the child was placed, covered with rich furs, and tied down with strong leather strings. The dust was changed as often as necessary till the child was weaned.

Among the Indians who are in any degree civilized, the women feed their children with pap made of Indian corn and milk, if it can be obtained, but in the parts more northern and remote from Europeans, wild rice and oats are substituted, which being cleansed from the husk and pounded between two stones, are boiled in water with maple sugar. This food is reckoned very nourishing, and with broth made from the flesh of animals and fish, which they are frequently able to procure, cannot fail of supporting and strengthening the infant. Among several of the tribes of Indians pap is made of sagavite, from a root they call toquo, of the bramble kind. This is washed and dried, afterward ground or pounded and made into a paste, which being baked is pleasant to the taste, but of a very astringent quality. It is their common bread.

II. GROWTH

The second age of man, said Shakespeare, was ". . . . the whining school-boy, with his satchel and shining morning face, creeping like snail unwillingly to school." Did the Indians have schools and colleges? Did they need them? Were Indian children nonetheless educated? By whom or what? Was Indian education adequate for Indian needs? What is education? Does it differ from culture to culture? Can the educational institutions of one culture be implanted successfully in another culture? Under what conditions, if any? Do modern societies have "initiation rites" comparable to the Delaware? What is the *social* function of these rites? Does the very existence of these rites say something about the cultural cohesiveness of the society?

Gabriel Sagard, The Long Journey to the Country of the Hurons, *ed. George M. Wrong (Toronto, 1939), pp. 132-134.*

The usual and daily practice of the young boys is none other than drawing the bow and shooting the arrow, making it rise and glide in a straight line a little higher than the ground. They play a game with curved sticks, making them slide over the snow and hit a ball of light wood, just as is done in our parts; they learn to throw the prong with which they spear fish, and practise other little sports and exercises, and then they put in an appearance at the lodge at meal-times, or else when they feel hungry. But if a mother asks her son to go for water or wood or do some similar household service, he will reply to her that this is a girl's work and will do none of it. If sometimes we got them to perform similar services it was on condition that they should always have access to our lodge, or for some pin, feather, or other little thing for adorning themselves, and this satisfied them very well, and us also, as a return for the small and petty services rendered us.

There were, however, some mischievous boys who delighted in cutting the cord that held up our door after the manner of the country, so as to make it fall when one opened it, and then afterwards they would deny it absolutely or take to flight. Moreover they never admit their faults or tricks, being great liars, except when they have no fear of being blamed or reproached for them, for though they are savages and incapable of receiving correction they are at the same time very proud and covetous of honour, and do not like to be thought mischievous or naughty, although they may be so.

We had made a beginning of teaching them their letters, but as they are all for freedom and only want to play and give themselves a good time, as I said, they forgot in three days what we had taken four to teach, for lack of perseverance and for neglect of coming back to us at the hours appointed them; and if they told us that they had been prevented because of a game, they were clear. Besides, it was not yet advisable to be severe with them or reprove them otherwise than gently, and we could only in a complaisant manner urge them to be thorough in gaining knowledge which would be such an advantage to them and bring them satisfaction in time to come.

Just as the little boys have their special training and teach one another to shoot with the bow as soon as they begin to walk, so also the little girls, whenever they begin to put one foot in front of the other, have a little stick put into their hands to train them and teach them early to pound corn, and when they are grown somewhat they also play various little games with their companions, and in the course of these small frolics they are trained quietly to perform trifling and petty household duties, sometimes also to do the evil that they see going on before their eyes, and this makes them worthless for the most part when grown up, and with few exceptions worse even than the boys, boasting often of the wickedness which should make them blush. They vie with one another as to which shall have the most lovers, and if the mother finds none for herself she freely offers her daughter and the daughter offers herself, and the husband also sometimes offers his wife, if she be willing, for some small and trifling present; and there are procurers and wicked people in the towns and villages who apply themselves to no other occupation than that of offering and bringing some of these creatures to the men who desire them. I give praises to our Lord that the women received our reproofs in quite good part, and finally began to practise modesty and show some shame at their dissoluteness, no longer venturing, except very rarely, to make use of improper language in our presence; and they were full of admiration and approval of the propriety of the girls in France of whom we told them. This gave us hopes of great amendment and alteration of their mode of living in a short time, if the Frenchmen who came up with us, most of them, had not told them the contrary, in order always to be able, like beasts, to enjoy their sensual pleasures to the full, in which they wallowed, even keeping together groups of these bad girls in several places, so that those who should have seconded us in teaching and being a good example to these people were the very ones who went about destroying and obstructing the good that we were building up for the salvation of the tribes and for the advancement of the glory of God. There were, however, some good men, virtuous and of good life, with whom we were well content and from whom we received spiritual encouragement, just as, on the contrary, we were scandalized by those other brutal, godless, and sensual men who hindered the conversion and amendment of these poor folk.

John Heckewelder (1743-1823), the English-born son of a Moravian minister, came to America in 1754. In 1762, he began to assist Moravian missionaries in their work with the Indians of Pennsylvania and Ohio, and for fifteen years (1771-1786) had his own mission in Ohio. After many years of study and life among the Indians, he was invited by the American Philosophical Society to publish his Account of the History, Manners, and Customs, of the Indian Natives who once inhabited Pennsylvania and the Neighbouring States *in the first volume of their* Transactions *(1819). The passage below comes from pp. 98-103 and 238-241 of that source.*

It may justly be a subject of wonder, how a nation without a written code of laws or system of jurisprudence, without any form or constitution of government, and without even a single elective or hereditary magistrate, can subsist together in peace and harmony, and in the exercise of the moral virtues; how a people can be well and effectually governed without any external authority; by the mere force of the ascendancy which men of superior minds have over those of a more ordinary stamp; by a tacit, yet universal submission to the aristocracy of experience, talents and virtue! Such, nevertheless, is the spectacle which an Indian nation exhibits to the eye of a stranger. I have been a witness to it for a long series of years, and after much observation and reflection to discover the cause of this phenomenon, I think I have reason to be satisfied that it is in a great degree to be ascribed to the pains which the Indians take to instil at an early age honest and virtuous principles upon the minds of their children, and to the method which they pursue in educating them. This method I will not call a system; for systems are unknown to these sons of nature, who, by following alone her simple dictates, have at once discovered and follow without effort that plain obvious path which the philosophers of Europe have been so long in search of.

The first step that parents take towards the education of their children, is to prepare them for future happiness, by impressing upon their tender minds, that they are indebted for their existence to a great, good and benevolent Spirit, who not only has given them life, but has ordained them for certain great purposes. That he has given them a fertile extensive country well stocked with game of every kind for their subsistence, and that by one of his inferior spirits he has also sent down to them from above corn, pumpkins, squashes, beans and other vegetables for their nourishment; all which blessings their ancestors have enjoyed for a great number of ages. That this great Spirit looks down upon the Indians, to see whether they are grateful to him and make him a due return for the many benefits he has bestowed, and therefore that it is their duty to show their thankfulness by worshipping him, and doing that which is pleasing in his sight.

This is in substance the first lesson taught, and from time to time repeated to the Indian children, which naturally leads them to reflect and gradually to understand that a being which hath done such great things for them, and all to make them happy, must be good indeed, and that it is surely their duty to do something that will please him.

They are then told that their ancestors, who received all this from the hands of the great Spirit, and lived in the enjoyment of it, must have been informed of what would be most pleasing to this good being, and of the manner in which his favour could be most surely obtained, and they are directed to look up for instruction to those who know all this, to learn from them, and revere them for their wisdom and the knowledge which they possess; this creates in the children a strong sentiment of respect for their elders, and a desire to follow their advice and example. Their young ambition is then excited by telling them that they were made the superiors of all other creatures, and are to have power over them; great pains are taken to make this feeling take an early root, and it becomes in fact their ruling passion through life; for no pains are spared to instil into them that by following the advice of the most admired and extolled hunter, trapper or warrior, they will at a future day acquire a degree of fame and reputation, equal to that which he possesses; that by submitting to the counsels of the aged, the chiefs, the men superior in wisdom, they may also rise to glory, and be called *Wisemen*, an honourable title, to which no Indian is indifferent. They are finally told that if they respect the aged and infirm, and are kind and obliging to them, they will be treated in the same manner when their turn comes to feel the infirmities of old age.

When this first and most important lesson is thought to be sufficiently impressed upon children's minds, the parents next proceed to make them sensible of the distinction between good and evil; they tell them that there are good actions and bad actions, both equally open to them to do or commit; that good acts are pleasing to the good Spirit which gave them their existence, and that on the contrary, all that is bad proceeds from the bad spirit who has given them nothing, and who cannot give them any thing that is good, because he has it not, and therefore he envies them that which they have received from the good Spirit, who is far superior to the bad one.

This introductory lesson, if it may be so called, naturally makes them wish to know what is good and what is bad. This the parent teaches him in his own way, that is to say, in the way in which he was himself taught by his own parents. It is not the lesson of an hour nor of a day, it is rather a long course more of practical than of theoretical instruction, a lesson, which is not repeated at stated seasons or times, but which is shown, pointed out, and demonstrated to the child, not only by those under whose immediate guardianship he is, but by the whole community, who consider themselves alike interested in the direction to be given to the rising generation.

When this instruction is given in the form of precepts, it must not be supposed that it is done in an authoritative or forbidding tone, but, on the contrary, in the gentlest and most persuasive manner: nor is the parent's authority ever supported by harsh or compulsive means; no whips, no punishments, no threats are even used to enforce commands or compel obedience. The child's *pride* is the feeling to which an appeal is made, which proves successful in almost every instance. A father needs only to say in the presence of his children: "I want such a thing done; I want one of my children to go upon such an errand; let me see who is the *good* child that will do it!" This word *good* operates, as it were, by magic, and the children immediately vie with each other to comply with the wishes of their parent. If a father sees an old decrepid man or woman pass by, led along by a child, he will draw the attention of his own children to the object by saying: "What a *good* child that must be, which pays such attention to the aged! That child, indeed, looks forward to the time when it will likewise be old!" or he will say, "May the great Spirit, who looks upon him, grant this *good* child a long life!"

In this manner of bringing up children, the parents, as I have already said, are seconded by the whole community. If a child is sent from his father's dwelling to carry a dish of victuals to an aged person, all in the house will join in calling him a *good* child. They will ask whose child he is, and on being told, will exclaim: what! has the *Tortoise*, or the *little Bear* (as the father's name may be) got such a *good* child? If a child is seen passing through the streets leading an old decrepid person, the villagers will in his hearing, and to encourage all the other children who may be present to take example from him, call on one another to look on and see what a *good* child that must be. And so, in most instances, this method is resorted to, for the purpose of instructing children in things that are good, proper, or honourable in themselves; while, on the other hand, when a child has committed a *bad* act, the parent will say to him: "O! how grieved I am that my child has done this *bad* act! I hope he will never do so again." This is generally effectual, particularly if said in the presence of others. The whole of the Indian plan of education tends to elevate rather than depress the mind, and by that means to make determined hunters and fearless warriors.

Thus, when a lad has killed his first game, such as a deer or a bear, parents who have boys growing up will not fail to say to some person in the presence of their own children: "That boy must have listened attentively to the aged hunters, for, though young, he has already given a proof that he will become a good hunter himself." If, on the other hand, a young man should fail of giving such a proof, it will be said of him "that he did not pay attention to the discourses of the aged."

In this indirect manner is instruction on all subjects given to the young people. They are to learn the arts of hunting, trapping, and making war, by listening to the aged when conversing together on those subjects, each, in his turn, relating how he acted, and opportunities are afforded to them for that purpose. By this mode of instructing youth, their respect for the aged is kept alive, and it is increased by the reflection that the same respect will be paid to them at a future day, when young persons will be attentive to what they shall relate.

This method of conveying instruction is, I believe, common to most Indian nations; it is so, at least, amongst all those that I have become acquainted with, and lays the foundation for that voluntary submission to their chiefs, for which they are so remarkable. Thus has been maintained for ages, without convulsions and without civil discords, this traditional government, of which the world, perhaps, does not offer another example; a government in which there are no positive laws, but only long established habits and customs, no code of jurisprudence, but the experience of former times, no magistrates, but advisers, to whom the people, nevertheless, pay a willing and implicit obedience, in which age confers rank, wisdom gives power, and moral goodness secures a title to universal respect. All this seems to be effected by the simple means of an excellent mode of education, by which a strong attachment to ancient customs, respect for age, and the love of virtue are indelibly impressed upon the minds of youth, so that these impressions acquire strength as time pursues its course, and as they pass through successive generations.

I do not know how to give a better name [*initiation*] to a

superstitious practice which is very common among the Indians, and, indeed, is universal among those nations that I have become acquainted with. By certain methods which I shall presently describe, they put the mind of a boy in a state of perturbation, so as to excite dreams and visions; by means of which they pretend that the boy receives instructions from certain spirits or unknown agents as to his conduct in life, that he is informed of his future destination and of the wonders he is to perform in his future career through the world.

When a boy is to be thus *initiated*, he is put under an alternate course of physic and fasting, either taking no food whatever, or swallowing the most powerful and nauseous medicines, and occasionally he is made to drink decoctions of an intoxicating nature, until his mind becomes sufficiently bewildered, so that he sees or fancies that he sees visions, and has extraordinary dreams, for which, of course, he has been prepared before hand. He will fancy himself flying through the air, walking under ground, stepping from one ridge or hill to the other across the valley beneath, fighting and conquering giants and monsters, and defeating whole hosts by his single arm. Then he has interviews with the Mannitto or with spirits, who inform him of what he was before he was born and what he will be after his death. His fate in this life is laid entirely open before him, the spirit tells him what is to be his future employment, whether he will be a valiant warrior, a mighty hunter, a doctor, a conjurer, or a prophet. There are even those who learn or pretend to learn in this way the time and manner of their death.

When a boy has been thus initiated, a name is given to him analogous to the visions that he has seen, and to the destiny that is supposed to be prepared for him. The boy, imagining all that happened to him while under perturbation, to have been real, sets out in the world with lofty notions of himself, and animated with courage for the most desperate undertakings.

The belief in the truth of those visions is universal among the Indians. I have spoken with several of their old men, who had been highly distinguished for their valour, and asked them whether they ascribed their achievements to natural or supernatural causes, and they uniformly answered, that as they knew beforehand what they could do, they did it of course. When I carried my questions farther, and asked them how they knew what they could do? they never failed

to refer to the dreams and visions which they had while under perturbation, in the manner I have above mentioned.

I always found it vain to attempt to undeceive them on this subject. They never were at a loss for examples to shew that the dreams
they had had were not the work of a heated imagination, but that
they came to them through the agency of a mannitto. They could always cite numerous instances of valiant men, who, in former times,
in consequence of such dreams, had boldly attacked their enemy with
nothing but the *Tamahican** [tomahawk] in their hand, had not
looked about to survey the number of their opponents, but had gone
straight forward, striking all down before them; some, they said, in
the French wars, had entered houses of the English filled with people, who, before they had time to look about, were all killed and laid
in a heap. Such was the strength, the power and the courage con-
veyed to them in their supernatural dreams, and which nothing could
resist.

If they stopped here in their relations, I might, perhaps, consider
this practice of putting boys under perturbation, as a kind of military
school or exercise, intended to create in them a more than ordinary
courage, and make them undaunted warriors. It certainly has this effect on some, who fancying themselves under the immediate protection of the celestial powers, despise all dangers, and really perform
acts of astonishing bravery. But it must be observed, that all that are
thus initiated are not designed for a military life, and that several
learn by their dreams that they are to be physicians, sorcerers, or that
their lives are to be devoted to some other *civil* employment. And it
is astonishing what a number of superstitious notions are infused into
the minds of the unsuspecting youth, by means of those dreams,
which are useless, at least, for making good warriors or hunters.
There are even some who by that means are taught to believe in the
transmigration of souls.

Benjamin Franklin needs no introduction. On 9 May 1753, he wrote a letter to Peter Collinson contrasting the Indian and the English ways of life. The following excerpt is taken from The Papers of Benjamin Franklin, *ed. Leonard W. Labaree* et al., *volume 4 (1961), pp. 482-483.*

The little value Indians set on what we prize so highly under the name of Learning appears from a pleasant passage that happened some years since at a Treaty between one of our Colonies and the Six Nations [Iroquois]; when every thing had been settled to the Satisfaction of both sides, and nothing remained but a mutual exchange of civilities, the English Commissioners told the Indians, they had in their Country a College for the instruction of Youth who were there taught various languages, Arts, and Sciences; that there was a particular foundation in favour of the Indians to defray the expense of the Education of any of their sons who should desire to take the Benefit of it. And now if the Indians would accept of the Offer, the English would take half a dozen of their brightest lads and bring them up in the Best manner; the Indians after consulting on the proposal replied that it was remembered some of their Youths had formerly been educated in that College, but it had been observed that for a long time after they returned to their Friends, they were absolutely good for nothing being neither acquainted with the true methods of killing deer, catching Beaver or surprizing an enemy. The Proposition, however, they looked on as a mark of the kindness and good will of the English to the Indian Nations which merited a grateful return; and therefore if the English Gentlemen would send a dozen or two of their Children to Onondago the great Council would take care of their Education, bring them up in really what was the best manner and make men of them.

III. LOVE AND MARRIAGE

Shakespeare's third stage of man was ". . . . the lover, sighing like furnace, with a woeful ballad made to his mistress' eyebrow." Were Indian men as smitten with their lovers? Did the Indians have engagements? divorces? What was the role of parents and relatives in the choice of marriage partners? Who made the final choice? Did Indians marry for convenience or love? Was premarital intercourse allowed? Was adultery? What was the nature of the marriage ceremony? What was required for a newly married couple to set up housekeeping? What were the conditions of a successful marriage? Did the Indians have more than one wife? If so, why? Were their marriages peaceful? long-lasting?

Chrestien Le Clercq, New Relation of Gaspesia, *ed. William F. Ganong (Toronto, 1910), pp. 259-264.*

The boys, according to the usual custom of the country, never leave the wigwams of their fathers except to go and live with some of their friends, where they hope to find girls whom they may marry. A boy has no sooner formed the design to espouse a girl than he makes for himself a proposal about it to her father, because he well knows that the girl will never approve the suit, unless it be agreeable to her father. The boy asks the father if he thinks it suitable for him to enter into his wigwam, that is to say, into relationship with him through marrying his daughter, for whom he professes to have much inclination. If the father does not like the suit of the young Indian, he tells him so without other ceremony than saying it cannot be; and this lover, however enamoured he may be, receives this reply with equanimity as the decisive decree of his fate and of his courtship, and seeks elsewhere some other sweetheart. It is not the same if the father finds that the suitor who presents himself is acceptable for his daughter; for then, after having given his consent to this lover, he tells him to speak to his sweetheart, in order to learn her wish about an affair which concerns herself alone. For they do not wish, say these barbarians, to force the inclinations of their children in the matter of marriage, or to induce them, whether by use of force, obedience, or affection, to marry men whom they cannot bring themselves to like. Hence it is that the fathers and mothers of our Gaspesians leave to their children the entire liberty of choosing the person whom they think most adaptable to their dispositions, and most conformable to their affections, although the parents, nevertheless, always keep the right to indicate to them the one whom they think most likely to be most suitable for them. But in the end this matter turns out only as those wish who are to be married; and they can very well say that they do not marry for the sake of others, but for themselves alone.

The boy, then, after obtaining the consent of the father, addresses himself to the girl, in order to ascertain her sentiments. He makes her a present from whatever important things he possesses; and the custom is such that if she is agreeable to his suit, she receives and accepts it with pleasure, and offers him in return some of her most beautiful workmanship. She takes care, say they, not to receive the least thing from those who seek her in marriage, in order not to contract any engagement with a young man whom she has not the intention of marrying.

The presents having been received and accepted by both parties, the Indian returns to his home, takes leave of his parents, and comes to live for an entire year in the wigwam of his sweetheart's father, whom, according to the laws of the country, he is to serve, and to whom he is to give all the furs which he secures in hunting. It is very much as formerly Jacob did, who served his father-in-law Laban before marrying Rachel. It is necessary then that he show himself a good hunter, capable of supporting a large family: that he make himself pleasant, obedient, and prompt to do everything which is connected with the welfare and the comfort of the wigwam: and that he be skilled in the usual exercises of the nation; this he does in order to

merit the esteem of his mistress and to make her believe that she will
be perfectly happy with him. The girl, for her part, also does her best
with that which concerns the housekeeping, and devotes herself
wholly, during this year, if the suit of the boy be pleasing to her, to
making snowshoes, sewing canoes, preparing barks, dressing skins of
moose or of beaver, drawing the sled—in a word, to doing everything
which can give her the reputation of being a good housewife.

As they are all equally poor and rich, self-interest never deter-
mines their marriages. Also there is never a question of dowry, of
property, of inheritance, of a contract, or of a notary who arranges
the property of the two parties in case of divorce. If they possess a
blanket, or some beaver robe, it is sufficient for setting up
housekeeping, and all that even the richest can hope for is a kettle, a
gun, a fire-steel, a knife, an axe, a canoe, and some other trifles.
These are all the riches of the newly-married couples, who do not
fail, nevertheless, to live content when this little is wanting, because
they hope to find in hunting that with which to supply in plenty their
needs and necessities.

Many persons are persuaded but too easily that the young man
abuses his future spouse during this year which he is obliged to spend
in the wigwam of his sweetheart. But aside from the fact that it is a
custom and an invariable law among our Gaspesians, which it is not
permissible to transgress without exposing the entire nation to some
considerable evil, it is truth to say that these two lovers live together
like brother and sister with much circumspection. I have never heard,
during all the time that I have lived in Gaspesia, that any disorder occurred between them, considering likewise that the women and the
girls, as we have said, are themselves so modest as not to permit in
this matter any liberty which would be contrary to their duty.

When, then, the two parties concur in disposition and tastes, at the
end of the year the oldest men of the nation, and the parents and
friends of the future married couple, are brought together to the feast
which is to be made for the public celebration of their marriage. The
young man is obliged to go for the provision, and the entertainment
is more or less magnificent according as he makes a hunt or a fishery
more or less successful. The usual speeches are made, they sing, they
dance, they amuse themselves; and in the presence of the whole
assembly the girl is given to the boy as his wife, without any other

ceremony. If it turns out then that the disposition of one is in-
compatible with the nature of the other, the boy or the girl retires
without fuss, and everybody is as content and satisfied as if the marriage had been accomplished, because, say they, one ought not to
marry only to be unhappy the remainder of one's days.

There is nevertheless much instability in these sorts of alliances,
and the young married folks change their inclinations very easily
when several years go by without their having children. "For in fact,"
say they to their wives, "I have only married thee in the hope of
seeing in my wigwam a numerous family, and since I cannot have
children with thee, let us separate, and seek elsewhere each his own
advantage." It is such that if any stability is found in the marriages of
our Gaspesians, it is only when the wife gives to her husband
evidence of her fecundity; and it can be said with truth that the children are then the indissoluble bonds, and the confirmation, of the
marriage of their father and mother, who keep faithful company
without ever separating, and who live in so great a union with one
another, that they seem not to have more than a single heart and a
single will. They are very fond of one another, and they agree
remarkably well. You never see quarrels, hatred, or reproaches
among them. The men leave the arrangements of the housekeeping to
the women, and do not interfere with them. The women cut up, slice
off, and give away the meat as they please, but the husband does not
get angry; and I can say that I have never seen the head of the
wigwam where I was living ask of his wife what had become of the
meat of moose and of beaver, although all that he had laid in had
diminished very quickly. No more have I ever heard the women complain because they were not invited to the feasts or the councils: because the men amused themselves and ate the best morsels: because
they themselves worked incessantly going to fetch wood for the fires,
building the wigwams, dressing the skins, and occupying themselves
with other severe labours, which are done only by the women. Each
does her little duty quietly, peaceably, and without debate. The mul-
tiplication of children does not embarrass them; the more they have,
the more they are content and satisfied.

One cannot express the grief of a Gaspesian when he loses his
wife. It is true that outwardly he dissimulates as much as he can the
bitterness which he has in his heart, because these people consider it

a mark of weakness unworthy of a man, be he ever so little brave and noble, to lament in public. If, then, the husband sometimes sheds tears, it is only to show that he is not insensible to the death of his wife, whom he loved tenderly; although it can truly be said that in his own privacy he abandons himself entirely to melancholy, which very often kills him, or which takes him to the most distant nations, there to make war and to drown in the blood of his enemies the sorrow and grief which overwhelm him.

Adriaen Van der Donck, A Description of the New Netherlands, *ed. Thomas F. O'Donnell (Syracuse, 1968), pp. 82-84.*

Marriages, and the fruits of marriage connections between males and females, keep up the succession of every living species in the world; and there has been no nation discovered or known, so barbarous as not to be benefited by marriage connections, and who have not upheld and supported the same. With the natives of the New Netherlands (for the Christian usages are the same as in Holland), we can still observe the old and ancient customs in their marriage ceremonies. But to illustrate the subject properly, it will be necessary to notice their distinguishing names of man and woman, father and mother, sister and brother, uncle and aunt, niece and nephew, husband and wife, married and unmarried, which are all known and distinguished among the natives by different and appropriate names, and give strong evidence of their attachment to their relatives, and of their preference to marriage connections. The natives generally marry but one wife, and no more, unless it be chief, who is great and powerful; such frequently have two, three, or four wives, of the neatest and handsomest women; and it is extraordinary, that the people can, by the light of nature, so effectually control their women, that no feuds or jealousies do arise and exist between them; for on inquiry, we have never discovered that any strife, hatred, or discord existed in an Indian family between the women about their family affairs, their children, or of the preference of their husband, whom they all esteem and implicitly obey. Concerning their marriages, they do not use as many ceremonies as the people of fashion do in Holland;

but they act more like common citizens on such occasions. With the natives there is no established time of marriageable years, but they judge their apparent fitness from their appearance, about which they are not very particular even to experimental proof. When the parties are young and related, the marriage usually takes place upon the counsel and advice of their relatives, having regard to their families and character. When the parties are widows or widowers, whether by death or otherwise, of whom there are many, then also it takes place sometimes upon the advice of friends; but it is not common for relatives to interfere in such marriages. The men, according to their condition, must always present their intended and betrothed bride with a marriage gift, as a confirmation of their agreement and of his intention, being similar to the marriage pledge of the ancients. When the parties are a widow or widower, who unite without the advice of friends, and the parties afterwards do not agree, for good cause or otherwise, then the husband frequently takes the gifts from his wife, forbids her his bed, and if she does not leave him, he turns her out of doors. Marriages with them are not so binding but that either party may altogether dissolve the union, which they frequently do. I have known an Indian who changed his wife every year, although he had little or no reason for it. We have also noticed that the dissolution of their marriages for unchastity arises more from the improper conduct of men than of the women. In their marriage dissolutions, the children follow their mother, which is also usual in many other nations who calculate their descent and genealogies from the mother's side. The longer a marriage exists among the natives, the more the parties are esteemed and honoured. To be unchaste during wedlock is held to be very disgraceful among them. Many of their women would prefer death, rather than submit to be dishonoured. Prostitution is considered baser by day than by night, and in the open fields than elsewhere, as it may be seen, or shined upon by the sun, which they say beholds the deed. No Indian will keep his wife, however much he loved her, when he knows she is unchaste. When their women are young, free, and unmarried, they act as they please, but they are always mercenary in their conduct, and deem it disgraceful to be otherwise; neither is the fruit of illicit connections despised, but the same are disregarded in a marriage connection. Few females will associate with men in a state of concubinage when they will not marry. Those women are proud of such conduct, and when they become old they will frequently boast of their connection with many of their chiefs and great men. This I have heard from several aged women, who deemed themselves honoured for having been esteemed, and gloried of their *"quasi bene gesta"* in their speeches. When one of their young women is *rijp* (for that is the native term), and wishes to be married, it is customary on such occasions that they veil their faces completely, and sit covered as an indication of their desire; whereupon propositions are made to such persons, and the practice is common with young women who have suitors, whereby they give publicity of their inclination. The men seldom make the first overtures, unless success is certain and they hope to improve their condition in life.

John Lawson, A New Voyage to Carolina *(Richmond, 1937), pp. 196-200.*

As for the Indian Marriages, I have read and heard of a great deal of Form and Ceremony used, which I never saw; nor yet could learn in the Time I have been amongst them, any otherwise than I shall here give you an Account of, which is as follows:

When any young Indian has a Mind for such a Girl to his Wife, he, or some one for him, goes to the young Woman's Parents, if living; if not, to her nearest Relations, where they make Offers of the Match betwixt the Couple. The Relations reply, they will consider of it; which serves for a sufficient Answer, till there be a second Meeting about the Marriage, which is generally brought into Debate before all the Relations, (that are old People) on both Sides, and sometimes the King with all his great Men, give their Opinions therein. If it be agreed on, and the young Woman approve thereof, (for these Savages never give their Children in Marriage without their own Consent) the Man pays so much for his Wife; and the handsomer she is the greater Price she bears. Now, it often happens, that the Man has not so much of their Money ready as he is to pay for his Wife; but if they know him to be a good Hunter, and that he can raise the Sum agreed for, in some few Moons, or any little time they agree, she shall go along with him as betrothed, but he is not to have any Knowledge of her till the utmost Payment is discharged; all which is punctually observed. Thus they lie together under one Covering for several Months, and the Woman remains the same as she was when she first came to him. I doubt our Europeans would be apt to break this Custom, but the Indian Men are not so vigorous and impatient in their Love as we are. Yet the Women are quite contrary, and those Indian Girls that have conversed with the English and other Europeans, never care for the Conversation of their own Countrymen afterwards.

They never marry so near as a first Cousin, and although there is nothing more coveted amongst them than to marry a Woman of their own Nation, yet when the Nation consists of a very few People, (as nowadays it often happens) so that they are all of them related to one another, then they look out for Husbands and Wives amongst Strangers. For if an Indian lies with his Sister, or any very near Relation, his Body is burnt, and his Ashes thrown into the River, as unworthy to remain on Earth; yet an Indian is allowed to marry two Sisters, or his Brother's Wife. Although these People are called Savages, yet Sodomy is never heard of amongst them, and they are so far from the Practice of that beastly and loathsome Sin, that they have no Name for it in their Language.

The Marriages of these Indians are no farther binding than the Man and Woman agree Together. Either of them has Liberty to leave the other upon any frivolous Excuse they can make, yet whosoever takes the Woman that was another Man's before, and bought by him, as they all are, must certainly pay to her former Husband whatsoever he gave for her. Nay, if she be a Widow, and her Husband died in Debt, whosoever takes her to Wife pays all her Husband's Obligations, though never so many; yet the Woman is not required to pay anything, (unless, she is willing) that was owing from her Husband, so long as she keeps Single. But if a Man courts her for a Night's Lodging and obtains it, the Creditors will make him pay her Husband's Debts, and he may, if he will take her for his Money, or sell her to another for his Wife. I have seen several of these Bargains driven in a day; for you may see Men selling their Wives as Men do Horses in a Fair, a Man being allowed not only to change as often as he pleases, but likewise to have as many Wives as he is able to maintain. I have often seen that very old Indian Men, (that have been Grandees in their own Nation) have had three or four very likely young Indian Wives, which I have much wandered at, because, to me they seemed incapacitated to make good Use of one of them.

The young Men will go in the Night from one House to another to visit the young Women, in which sort of Rambles they will spend the whole Night. In their Addresses they find no Delays, for if she is willing to entertain the Man, she gives him Encouragement and grants him Admittance; otherwise she withdraws her Face from him, and says, I cannot see you, either you or I must leave this Cabin and sleep somewhere else this Night.

They are never to boast of their Intrigues with the Women. If they do, none of the Girls value them ever after, or admit of their Company in their Beds. This proceeds not on the score of Reputation, for there is no such thing, (on that account) known amongst them; and although we may reckon them the greatest Libertines and most extravagant in their Embraces, yet they retain and possess a Modesty that requires those Passions never to be divulged.

The Trading Girls, after they have led that Course of Life, for several Years, in which time they scarce ever have a Child; (for they have an Art to destroy the Conception, and she that brings a Child in this Station, is accounted a Fool, and her Reputation is lessened thereby) at last they grow weary of so many, and betake themselves to a married State, or to the Company of one Man; neither does their having been common to so many any wise lessen their Fortunes, but rather augment them.

The Woman is not punished for Adultery, but tis the Man that makes the injured Person Satisfaction, which is the Law of Nations practised amongst them all; and he that strives to evade such Satisfaction as the Husband demands, lives daily in Danger of his Life; yet when discharged, all Animosity is laid aside, and the Cuckold is very well pleased with his Bargain, whilst the Rival is laughed at by the whole Nation, for carrying on his intrigue with no better Conduct, than to be discovered and pay so dear for his Pleasure.

The Indians say, that the Woman is a weak Creature, and easily drawn away by the Man's Persuasion; for which Reason, they lay no Blame upon her, but the Man (that ought to be Master of his Passion) for persuading her to it.

They are of a very hale Constitution; their Breaths are as Sweet as the Air they breathe in, and the Woman seems to be of that tender Composition, as if they were designed rather for the Bed than Bondage. Yet their Love is never of that Force and Continuance, that any of them ever runs Mad, or makes away with themselves on that score. They never love beyond Retrieving their first Indifferency, and when slighted, are as ready to untie the Knot at one end, as you are at the other.

Yet I knew an European Man that had a Child or two by one of these Indian Women, and afterwards married a Christian, after which he came to pass away a Night with his Indian Mistress; but she made Answer that she then had forgot she ever knew him, and that she never lay with another Woman's Husband, so fell a crying and took up the Child she had by him, and went out of the Cabin (away from him) in great Disorder.

John Heckewelder, An Account of the History, Manners, and Customs, of the Indian Nations, who once Inhabited Pennsylvania and the Neighbouring States, *in* Transactions of the American Philosophical Society, *volume 1 (1819), pp. 142-152.*

There are many persons who believe, from the labour that they see the Indian women perform, that they are in a manner treated as slaves. These labours, indeed, are hard, compared with the tasks that are imposed upon females in civilised society; but they are no more than their fair share, under every consideration and due allowance, of the hardships attendant on savage life. Therefore they are not only voluntarily, but cheerfully submitted to; and as women are not obliged to live with their husbands any longer than suits their pleasure or convenience, it cannot be supposed that they would submit to be loaded with unjust or unequal burdens.

Marriages among the Indians are not, as with us, contracted for life; it is understood on both sides that the parties are not to live together any longer than they shall be pleased with each other. The husband may put away his wife whenever he pleases, and the woman may in like manner abandon her husband. Therefore the connexion is not attended with any vows, promises or ceremonies of any kind. An Indian takes a wife as it were on trial, determined, however, in

his own mind not to forsake her if she behaves well, and particularly
if he has children by her. The woman, sensible of this, does on her
part everything in her power to please her husband, particularly if he
is a good hunter or trapper, capable of maintaining her by his skill
and industry, and protecting her by his strength and courage.

When a marriage takes place, the duties and labours incumbent on
each party are well known to both. It is understood that the husband
is to build a house for them to dwell in, to find the necessary imple-
ments of husbandry, as axes, hoes, &c. to provide a canoe, and also
dishes, bowls, and other necessary vessels for house-keeping. The
woman generally has a kettle or two, and some other articles of
kitchen furniture, which she brings with her. The husband, as master of
the family, considers himself bound to support it by his bodily exertions, as hunting, trapping, &c.; the woman, as his *help-mate*, takes
upon herself the labours of the field, and is far from considering them
as more important than those to which her husband is subjected,
being well satisfied that with his gun and traps he can maintain a
family in any place where game is to be found: nor do they think it
any hardship imposed upon them; for they themselves say, that while
their field labour employs them at most six weeks in the year, that of
the men continues the whole year round.

When a couple is newly married, the husband (without saying a
single word upon the subject) takes considerable pains to please his
wife, and by repeated proofs of his skill and abilities in the art of
hunting, to make her sensible that she can be happy with him, and
that she will never want while they live together. At break of day he
will be off with his gun, and often by breakfast time return home with
a deer, turkey, or some other game. He endeavours to make it appear
that it is in his power to bring provisions home whenever he pleases,
and his wife, proud of having such a good hunter for her husband,
does her utmost to serve and make herself agreeable to him.

The work of the women is not hard or difficult. They are both
able and willing to do it, and always perform it with cheerfulness.
Mothers teach their daughters those duties which common sense
would otherwise point out to them when grown up. Within doors,
their labour is very trifling; there is seldom more than one pot or kettle to attend to. There is no scrubbing of the house, and but little to
wash, and that not often. Their principal occupations are to cut and

fetch in the fire wood, till the ground, sow and reap the grain, and pound the corn in mortars for their pottage, and to make bread which they bake in the ashes. When going on a journey, or to hunting camps with their husbands, if they have no horses, they carry a pack on their backs which often appears heavier than it really is; it generally consists of a blanket, dressed deer skin for mocksens, a few articles of kitchen furniture, as a kettle, bowl or dish, with spoons and some bread, corn, salt, &c. for their nourishment. I have never known an Indian woman complain of the hardship of carrying this burden, which serves for their own comfort and support as well as of their husbands.

The tilling of the ground at home, getting of the fire wood, and pounding of corn in mortars, is frequently done by female parties, much in the manner of those husking, quilting and other *frolics* (as they are called,) which are so common in some parts of the United States, particularly to the eastward. The labour is thus quickly and easily performed; when it is over, and sometimes in intervals, they sit down to enjoy themselves by feasting on some good victuals, prepared for them by the person or family for whom they work, and which the man has taken care to provide before hand from the woods; for this is considered a principal part of the business, as there are generally more or less of the females assembled who have not, perhaps for a long time, tasted a morsel of meat, being either widows, or orphans, or otherwise in straitened circumstances. Even the chat which passes during their joint labours is highly diverting to them, and so they seek to be employed in this way as long as they can, by going round to all those in the village who have ground to till.

When the harvest is in, which generally happens by the end of September, the women have little else to do than to prepare the daily victuals, and get fire wood, until the latter end of February or beginning of March, as the season is more or less backward, when they go to their sugar camps, where they extract sugar from the maple tree. The men having built or repaired their temporary cabin, and made all the troughs of various sizes, the women commence making sugar, while the men are looking out for meat, at this time generally fat bears, which are still in their winter quarters. When at home, they will occasionally assist their wives in gathering the sap, and watch the kettles in their absence, that the syrup may not boil over.

A man who wishes his wife to be with him while he is out hunting in the woods, needs only tell her, that on such a day they will go to such a place, where he will hunt for a length of time, and she will be sure to have provisions and everything else that is necessary in complete readiness, and well packed up to carry to the spot; for the man, as soon as he enters the woods, has to be looking out and about for game, and therefore cannot be encumbered with any burden; after wounding a deer, he may have to pursue it for several miles, often running it fairly down. The woman, therefore, takes charge of the baggage, brings it to the place of encampment, and there, immediately enters on the duties of housekeeping, as if they were at home; she moreover takes pains to dry as much meat as she can, that none may be lost; she carefully puts the tallow up, assists in drying the skins, gathers as much wild hemp as possible for the purpose of making strings, carrying bands, bags and other necessary articles, collects roots for dyeing; in short does every thing in her power to leave no care to her husband but the important one of providing meat for the family.

After all, the fatigue of the women is by no means to be compared to that of the men. Their hard and difficult employments are periodical and of short duration, while their husband's labours are constant and severe in the extreme. Were a man to take upon himself a part of his wife's duty, in addition to his own, he must necessarily sink under the load, and of course his family must suffer with him. On his exertions as a hunter, their existence depends; in order to be able to follow that rough employment with success, he must keep his limbs as supple as he can, he must avoid hard labour as much as possible, that his joints may not become stiffened, and that he may preserve the necessary strength and agility of body to enable him to pursue the chase, and bear the unavoidable hardships attendant on it; for the fatigues of hunting wear out the body and constitution far more than manual labour. Neither creeks nor rivers, whether shallow or deep, frozen or free from ice, must be an obstacle to the hunter, when in pursuit of a wounded deer, bear, or other animal, as is often the case. Nor has he then leisure to think on the state of his body, and to consider whether his blood is not too much heated to plunge without danger into the cold stream, since the game he is in pursuit of is running off from him with full speed. Many dangerous accidents often befal him, both as a hunter and a warrior, (for he is both) and are seldom unattended with painful consequences, such as rheumatism or consumption of the lungs, for which the sweat-house, on which they so much depend, and to which they often resort for relief, especially after a fatiguing hunt or warlike excursion, is not always a sure preservative or an effectual remedy.

The husband generally leaves the skins and peltry which he has procured by hunting to the care of his wife, who sells or barters them away to the best advantage for such necessaries as are wanted in the family; not forgetting to supply her husband with what he stands in need of, who, when he receives it from her hands never fails to return her thanks in the kindest manner. If debts had been previously contracted, either by the woman, or by her and her husband jointly, or if a horse should be wanted, as much is laid aside as will be sufficient to pay the debts or purchase the horse.

When a woman has got in her harvest of corn, it is considered as belonging to her husband, who, if he has suffering friends, may give them as much of it as he pleases, without consulting his wife, or being afraid of her being displeased; for she is in the firm belief that he is able to procure that article whenever it is wanted. The sugar which she makes out of the maple tree is also considered as belonging to her husband.

There is nothing in an Indian's house or family without its particular owner. Every individual knows what belongs to him, from the horse or cow down to the dog, cat, kitten and little chicken. Parents make presents to their children, and they in return to their parents. A father will sometimes ask his wife or one of his children for the loan of his horse to go out a hunting. For a litter of kittens or brood of chickens, there are often as many different owners as there are individual animals. In purchasing a hen with her brood, one frequently has to deal for it with several children. Thus, while the principle of community of goods prevails in the state, the rights of property are acknowledged among the members of a family. This is attended with a very good effect; for by this means every living creature is properly taken care of. It also promotes liberality among the children, which becomes a habit with them by the time they are grown up.

An Indian loves to see his wife well clothed, which is a proof that he is fond of her; at least, it is so considered. While his wife is bartering the skins and peltry he has taken in his hunt, he will seat himself at some distance, to observe her choice, and how she and the traders agree together. When she finds an article which she thinks will suit or please her husband, she never fails to purchase it for him; she tells him that it is *her* choice, and he is never dissatisfied.

The more a man does for his wife, the more he is esteemed, particularly by the women, who will say: "This man surely loves his wife." Some men at their leisure hours make bowls and ladles, which, when finished, are at their wives' disposal.

If a sick or pregnant woman longs for any article of food, be it what it may, and however difficult to be procured, the husband immediately sets out to endeavour to get it. I have known a man to go forty or fifty miles for a mess of cranberries to satisfy his wife's longing. In the year 1762, I was witness to a remarkable instance of the disposition of Indians to indulge their wives. There was a famine in the land, and a sick Indian woman expressed a great desire for a mess of Indian corn. Her husband having heard that a trader at Lower Sandusky had a little, set off on horseback for that place, one hundred miles distant, and returned with as much corn as filled the crown of his hat, for which he gave his horse in exchange, and came home on foot, bringing his saddle back with him. Squirrels, ducks, and other like delicacies, when most difficult to be obtained, are what women in the first stage of their pregnancy generally long for. The husband in every such case will go out and spare no pains nor trouble until he has procured what is wanted.

In other cases, the men and their wives do not in general trouble themselves with each other's business; but the wife, knowing that the father is very fond of his children, is always prepared to tell him some diverting anecdote of one or the other of them, especially if he has been absent for some time.

It very seldom happens that a man condescends to quarrel with his wife, or abuse her, though she has given him just cause. In such a case the man, without replying, or saying a single word, will take his gun and go into the woods, and remain there a week or perhaps a fortnight, living on the meat he has killed, before he returns home again; well knowing that he cannot inflict a greater punishment on his wife for her conduct to him than by absenting himself for a while; for she is not only kept in suspense, uncertain whether he will return again, but is soon reported as a bad and quarrelsome woman; for, as on those occasions, the man does not tell his wife on what day or at what time he will be back again, which he otherwise, when they are on good terms, never neglects to do, she is at once put to shame by her neighbours, who soon suspecting something, do not fail to put such questions to her, as she either cannot, or is ashamed to answer. When he at length does return, she endeavours to let him see by her attentions, that she has repented, though neither speak to each other a single word on the subject of what has passed. And as his children, if he has any, will on his return hang about him and soothe him with their caresses, he is, on their account, ready to forgive, or at least to say nothing unpleasant to their mother. She has, however, received by this a solemn warning, and must take care how she behaves in future, lest the next time her husband should stay away altogether and take another wife. It is very probable, that if at this time they had had no children, he would have left her, but then he would have taken his property with him at the same time.

On the return of an Indian from a journey, or long absence, he will on entering the house, say, "I am returned!" to which his wife will reply, "I rejoice!" and having cast his eyes around, he will enquire, whether all the children are well, when being answered in the affirmative, he replies, "I am glad!" which for the present is all the conversation that passes between them; nor does he relate any thing at this present time that occurred on his journey, but holds himself in readiness to partake of the nourishment which his wife is preparing for him. After a while, when the men of the village have assembled at his house, his wife, with the rest, hears his story at full length.

Marriages are proposed and concluded in different ways. The parents on both sides, having observed an attachment between two young persons, negotiate for them. This generally commences from the house where the bridegroom lives, whose mother is the negotiatrix for him, and begins her duties by taking a good leg of venison, or bear's meat, or something else of the same kind, to the house where the bride dwells, not forgetting to mention, that her son has killed it: in return for this the mother of the bride, if she otherwise approves of the match, which she well understands by the presents to be intended, will prepare a good dish of victuals, the produce of the labour of *woman*, such as beans, Indian corn, or the like, and then taking it to the house where the bridegroom lives, will say, "This is the produce of my daughter's field;" and she also prepared it. If afterwards the mothers of the parties are enabled to tell the good news to each other, that the young people have pronounced that which was sent them *very good*, the bargain is struck. It is as much as if the young man had said to the girl, "I am able to provide you at all times with meat to eat!" and she had replied, "and such good victuals from the field, you shall have from me!" From this time not only presents of this kind are continued on both sides, but articles of clothing are presented to the parents by each party, by way of return for what they have received, of which the young people always have a share. The friendship between the two families daily increasing, they do their domestic and field work jointly, and when the young people have agreed to live together, the parents supply them with necessaries, such as a kettle, dishes or bowls, and also what is re-quired for the kitchen, and with axes, hoes, &c. to work in the field.

The men who have no parents to negotiate for them, or otherwise choose to manage the matter for themselves, have two simple ways of attaining their object. The first is: by stepping up to the woman whom they wish to marry, saying: "If you are willing I will take you as wife!" when if she answer in the affirmative, she either goes with him immediately, or meets him at an appointed time and place.

The other mode of celebrating marriage will appear from the following anecdote.

An aged Indian, who for many years had spent much of his time among the white people both in Pennsylvania and New Jersey, one day about the year 1770 observed, that the Indians had not only a much easier way of getting a wife than the whites, but were also more certain of getting a *good* one; "For," (said he in his broken English,) "White man court,—court,—may be one whole year!—may be two year before he marry!—well!—may be then got *very good* wife—but may be *not!*—may be *very* cross!—Well now, suppose cross! scold so soon as get awake in the morning! scold all day! scold until sleep!—all one; he must keep *him!* [The Indian language has no feminine form of the pronoun.] White people have law forbidding throwing away wife, be *he* ever so cross! must keep *him* always! Well! how does Indian do?—Indian when he see industrious Squaw, which he like, he go to *him*, place his two forefingers close aside each other, make two look like one—look Squaw in the face—see *him* smile—which is all one *he* say, *Yes!* so he take *him* home—no danger *he* be cross! no! no! Squaw know too well what Indian do if *he* cross!—throw *him* away and take another! Squaw love to eat meat! no husband! no meat! Squaw do every thing to please husband! he do the same to please Squaw! live happy!''

IV. WORK AND PLAY

The Europeans who came to America were the products of a Christian culture that placed a high premium on effort and hard work. When they looked at the Indian way of life, what did they see? Were the Indians lazy? By whose standards? In the context of their own culture, were they lazy? How much work was required to maintain Indian life? What were the chief occupations of the Indians? Did the work of men and women differ? What forms of recreation did they enjoy? Were these appropriate to their culture? Are our games appropriate to modern society? To what extent are children's games playful preparations for adult life?

Gabriel Sagard, The Long Journey to the Country of the Hurons, *ed. George M. Wrong (Toronto, 1939), pp. 96-109.*

The occupations of the savages are fishing, hunting, and war; going off to trade, making lodges and canoes, or contriving the proper tools for doing so. The rest of the time they pass in idleness, gambling, sleeping, singing, dancing, smoking, or going to feasts, and they are reluctant to undertake any other work that forms part of the women's duty except under strong necessity.

Gambling is so frequent and customary a practice with them that it takes up much of their time, and sometimes not only the men but the women also stake all they possess, and lose as cheerfully and patiently, when chance does not favour them, as if they had lost nothing. I have seen some of them going back to their villages quite naked and singing, after having left everything in the hands of one of our people, and it happened once that a Canadian lost both wife and children at play with a Frenchman; they were, however, given back to him afterwards voluntarily. The men are addicted not only to the game of straws, called *Aescara*, for which three or four hundred little white reeds are cut of equal length, a foot long or thereabouts, but also to many other kinds of play. One is to have a large wooden bowl and put into it five or six fruit-stones or little balls slightly flattened, as big as the tip of your little finger, and painted black on one side and white or yellow on the other; and when they are all squatting on the ground in a circle, their accustomed posture, they take this bowl in turn, according to lot, in both hands, lift it a little from the ground, and at once replace it, giving it rather a sharp knock so that the little balls are made to move and leap up, and then, as in dicing, they see on which side the balls lie, and if it is in their favour. The one who holds the bowl, while he is jolting it and looking at his throw, keeps saying without a pause *Tet, tet, tet, tet*, thinking that this affects the throw and makes it a favourable one for him. But the special game of the women and girls, in which also men and boys sometimes take part with them, is played with five or six fruit-stones like those of our apricots, blackened on one side. They hold them in their hand, as one does dice, then cast them upward a little, and, when they have fallen on a piece of leather or skin stretched on the ground for the purpose, see what the throw gives them; and they keep on at it, trying to win collars, ear-rings, or other trifles they possess, but never money, for of that they have neither knowledge nor use, but offer and give one thing in exchange for another throughout the whole of the savages' country.

I must not omit to mention also that in some of their villages they practise what we in France call "porter les momons". They challenge and invite the other towns and villages to come to see them, to gamble with them and win their very utensils if it should so turn out, and while this goes on there is no lack of feasting. For on the slightest occasion the kettle is always ready, especially in winter, which is the time when they chiefly feast one another. They are fond of painting, and practise it with considerable skill, considering that they have no rules of art nor fitting means; yet they make pictures of men, animals, birds, and other things in caricature, both in perspective on stones, wood, and other similar substances, and painted flat upon their bodies. They make these not for idolatry, but to enjoy looking at them, as an ornament for their calumets and pipes and to decorate the front of their lodges.

During winter with the twine twisted by the women and girls they make nets and snares for fishing and catching fish in summer, and even in winter under the ice by means of lines or the seine-net, through holes cut in several places. They make also arrows with the knife, very straight and long, and when they have no knives they use sharp-edged stones; they fledge them with feathers from the tails and wings of eagles, because these are strong and carry well in the air, and at the point with strong fish-glue they attach sharp-pointed stones or bones, or iron heads obtained in trade from the French. They make also wooden clubs for warfare, and shields which cover almost the whole body, and with animals' guts they make bow-strings and rackets for walking on the snow when they go for wood and to hunt.

They make journeys overland too, as well as by sea and river, and they will undertake (an incredible thing) to go for ten, twenty, thirty, and forty leagues through the woods where they find neither paths nor houses, and without carrying any provisions, but only tobacco and steel, with their bow in their hand and quiver at their back. If they have an urgent thirst and no water they know how to suck it from the trees, and in particular from beech-trees, out of which distils a sweet and very pleasant liquid at the time when the trees are in sap, as we also did. But when they undertake journeys to distant countries they do not usually make them except after due consideration nor without having received permission from the chiefs. These in a special council are in the habit of determining every year the number of men who may go out from each town or village, so as not to leave them unprovided with warriors, and anyone who wishes to go away without this authorization may do so to be sure, but he will be blamed and thought foolish and imprudent. I have seen several savages from neighbouring villages come to Quieunonascaran to ask leave of absence from Onorotandi, brother of the great chief Auoindaon, in order that they might have permission to go to the Saguenay. For he is called the Master and Overlord of the roads and rivers that lead there, that is, up to the limits of the Huron country. Similarly it was necessary to get permission from Auoindaon to go to Quebec, and since each means to be master in his own country, they allow no

one of another tribe of savages to pass through their country to go to
the trading unless they are recognized as master and their favour
secured by a present. No difficulty is made of this by the others;
without it they might be hindered or an injury done to them.

In winter when the fish feel the cold and withdraw [to deep water]
the nomad savages, such as the Canadians, Algonquins, and others,
leave the shores of the sea and the rivers, and encamp in the woods,
wherever they know there is game. As to our Hurons, the Hon-
queronons, and [other] sedentary peoples, they do not quit their
lodges nor move their towns and villages . . . When the nomad tribes
are hungry they consult the oracle, and then go off, bow in hand and
quiver at their back, in the direction that their Oki has pointed out to
them, or elsewhere where they think they will not be wasting their
time. They have dogs which follow them, and although these do not
bark, yet they understand quite well how to discover the lair of the
animal they are looking for. When it is found the men pursue it
courageously and never leave it until they have brought it down;
finally, having wearied it to death they get their dogs to worry it so
that it must fall. Then they cut open the belly, give the quarry to the
dogs, have a feast, and carry off the remainder. If the animal, too
hard pressed, comes to a river, the sea, or a lake, it leaps into it
boldly; but the savages, active and ready, are immediately after it in
their canoes, if there are any at hand, and then give it the death-
stroke.

Their canoes are from eight to nine paces in length and about a
pace or a pace and a half wide at the middle, tapering off to both
ends like a weaver's shuttle, and these are the largest they make.
They have also others smaller, which they use as occasion requires
and according to the difficulty of the journeys they have to make.
The canoes are very liable to turn over if one does not understand
how to manage them, being made of birchbark strengthened within
by little hoops of white cedar, very neatly placed, and they are so
light that a man can easily carry one on his head or on his shoulder.
Each can support the weight of a hogshead, more or less according to
its size. Every day as a rule when they are in a hurry they do twenty-
five or thirty leagues in these canoes, provided that there is no rapid
to pass and that wind and water are favourable; for they go at such
speed and with such lightness as astonished me, and I do not think

the mail can go more quickly than these canoes, when they are driven by good paddlers.

Just as the men have their special occupation and understand wherein a man's duty consists, so also the women and girls keep their place and perform quietly their little tasks and functions of service. They usually do more work than the men, although they are not forced or compelled to do so. They have the care of the cooking and the household, of sowing and gathering corn, grinding flour, preparing hemp and tree-bark, and providing the necessary wood. And because there still remains plenty of time to waste, they employ it in gaming, going to dances and feasts, chatting and killing time, and doing just what they like with their leisure; this is no trifle, since their whole household arrangements amount to but little, in view furthermore of the fact that among our Hurons they are not admitted to many of the men's feasts nor to any of their councils, nor allowed to put up lodges and make canoes. They have discovered how to twist hemp thread on the thigh, not using distaff and spindle, and with this thread the men twine their nets and snares as I have said. They also pound corn for cooking and roast it in hot ashes. Again, they extract the meal for their husbands when these go in summer to trade with other nations far away.

They make pottery, especially round pots without handles or feet, in which they cook their food, meat or fish. When winter comes they make mats of reeds, which they hang in the doors of their lodges, and they make others to sit upon, all very neatly. The women of the High Hairs, moreover, colour the reeds and make divisions in the weaving in such apt proportion that no fault can be found with it. They dress and soften the skins of beaver and moose and others, as well as we could do it here, and of these they make their cloaks and coverings; and they paint them in patterns and a mixture of colours with very good effect. Likewise they make reed baskets, and others out of birchbark, to hold beans, corn, and peas (which they call *Acointa*), meat, fish, and other small provender. They also make a kind of leather game-bag or tobacco-pouch, which they work in a manner worthy of admiration with porcupine quills, coloured red, black, white, and blue, and these colours they make so bright that ours do not seem to come near them in that respect. They employ themselves also in making bowls of bark for drinking and eating out of, and for holding their meats and soups. Moreover the sashes, collars, and bracelets that they and the men wear are of their workmanship; and in spite of the fact that they are more occupied than the men, who play the noblemen among them and think only of hunting, fishing, or fighting, still they usually love their husbands better than the women here. If they were Christians these would be families among whom God would take pleasure to dwell.

It is their custom for every family to live on its fishing, hunting, and planting, since they have as much land as they need; for all the forests, meadows, and uncleared land are common property, and anyone is allowed to clear and sow as much as he will and can, and according to his needs; and this cleared land remains in his possession for as many years as he continues to cultivate and make use of it. After it is altogether abandoned by its owner, then anyone who wishes uses it, but not otherwise. Clearing is very troublesome for them, since they have no proper tools. They cut down the trees at the height of two or three feet from the ground, then they strip off all the branches, which they burn at the stump of the same trees in order to kill them, and in course of time they remove the roots. Then the women clean up the ground between the trees thoroughly, and at distances a pace apart dig round holes or pits. In each of these they sow nine or ten grains of maize, which they have first picked out, sorted, and soaked in water for a few days, and so they keep on until they have sown enough to provide food for two or three years, either for fear that some bad season may visit them or else in order to trade it to other nations for furs and other things they need; and every year they sow their corn thus in the same holes and spots, which they freshen with their little wooden spade, shaped like an ear with a handle at the end. The rest of the land is not tilled, but only cleansed of noxious weeds, so that it seems as if it were all paths, so careful are they to keep it quite clean; and this made me, as I went alone sometimes from one village to another, lose my way usually in these corn-fields more than in the meadows and forests.

Now the corn being thus sown in the manner in which we sow beans there comes up from a single grain only one shoot or stalk, and the stalk bears two or three ears, each ear yielding a hundred, two hundred, sometimes four hundred grains, and there are some which yield more. The stalk grows as high as a man and higher, and is very

thick. It does not grow so well and so high, nor is the ear so big or the
grain so good, in Canada or France as there. The grain ripens in four
months, or in three in some places. After that they gather it, and
turning the leaves up and tying them round the ears arrange it in
bundles hung in rows, the whole length of the lodge from top to bottom, on poles which they put up as a sort of rack, coming down as
low as to the edge of the roof in front of the bench, and all so neatly
disposed that it looks like tapestry draped the whole length of the
lodge. When the grain is quite dry and fit for storing the women and
girls shell it, clean it, and put it into their great vats or casks made for
the purpose and placed in the porch or in some corner of the lodge.

In order to eat it in the form of bread, they first boil the grain for a
short time in water, then wipe it and dry it a little; after that they
crush it and knead it with warm water and bake it, wrapped up in
corn-leaves; if no leaves have been put round it they wash it after it is
baked. If they have any beans they cook them in a small pot and mix
them in the dough without crushing them, or else strawberries,
blueberries, raspberries, blackberries, and other small fruits, dried
and fresh, to give it taste and improve it; for by itself, without a mixture of these small relishes, it is very insipid. This bread, and any
other kind of biscuit we use, they call *Andataroni*, with the exception
of the bread shaped and prepared like two balls joined together,
which is wrapped in leaves of the Indian corn, then boiled and
cooked in water, not baked under the ashes: to this they give a special name, *Coinkia*. Again, they make another kind of bread: they
gather a number of ears of corn before it is thoroughly dry and ripe,
and then the women, girls, and children bite off the grains, spitting
them out of their mouths afterwards into large pots which they keep
beside them, and then they finish by pounding it in a large mortar;
and since this paste is very soft they must necessarily wrap it in
leaves in order to bake it under the ashes in the usual way. This
chewed bread is the kind they themselves prize most, but for my part
I only ate it of necessity and reluctantly, because the corn had in this
way been half chewed, bruised, and kneaded by the teeth of the
women, girls, and little children.

Maize bread, with the *sagamite* made from it, is of very good
substance, and I was surprised that it supplied such excellent
nourishment as it does; for, though drinking only water in that coun-

try, and eating this bread only very seldom, and meat even more rarely, and taking almost nothing but *sagamité* alone, with a very small quantity of fish, one keeps well and in good condition, provided that one has enough of it; and there is no scarcity of it while one lives in the country, but only on long journeys, in which one often suffers greatly from want.

They introduce variety into the preparation of their corn for eating in many ways; for just as we invent different sauces to indulge our appetite, so they also take pains to make their broth in different ways, so as to enjoy it better, and the way which seemed to me most agreeable was *Neintahouy*, after that *Eschionque*. *Neintohouy* is made in this manner. The women roast a number of ears of corn before they are quite ripe, keeping them propped up against a stick resting on two stones before the fire, and turn one side and then the other until they are sufficiently roasted, or, in order to get them done the quicker, thrust them into a heap of sand, which has first been well heated by a good fire on top of it, and take them out again; then they strip off the grains and spread these out on bark to dry still further in the sun. After it is dry enough they store it in a cask along with a third or a quarter as much of their beans, called *Ogaressa*, mixing them up with it; and when they wish to eat it they boil it whole in their pot or kettle, which they call *Anoo*, along with a little meat or fish, fresh or dried, if they have any. To make *Eschionque* they roast on the ashes of their hearth mixed with sand a quantity of dried corn, like peas, then they pound this maize very small, and next with a little fan of tree-bark they take away the fine flour, and this is *Eschionque*. This meal is eaten dry as well as cooked in a pot, or else steeped in water, warm or cold. When they wish to have it cooked they put it in the broth into which they have first minced and boiled some meat or fish, together with a quantity of pumpkin, if they like, or they put it into quite clear broth, and enough of it to make the *sagamité* sufficiently thick. They keep stirring it with a spatula, called by them *Estoqua*, for fear of it sticking together in lumps; and immediately after it has boiled a little they pour it into the bowls, with a little oil or melted fat, if they have any, on top of it. This *sagamité* is quite good and very satisfying. The hull of this flour which they call *Acointa*, that is peas (for they give it the same name as they do our peas), they boil separately in water with fish, if there is any, and then eat it.

They do the same with corn that has not been pounded, but it is very hard to cook. The ordinary *sagamité,* which they call *Ottet*, is raw maize ground into meal, without separating the flour from the hull, boiled very clear, with a little meat or fish if they have any. They also sometimes put in pumpkin cut up into small pieces, if it is in season, and quite often nothing at all. For fear the meal may stick to the bottom of the pot they stir it frequently with the *Estoqua*, and then eat it; it is the soup, meat, and dessert of every day, and there is nothing more to expect at the meal, for even when they have some trifle of meat or fish to share among them (which rarely happens except at the hunting or fishing season) it is divided and eaten first, before the soup or *sagamité*.

To make *Leindohy*, or stinking corn, a large number of ears of corn are used, and those not yet at all dry and ripe, so that they may be more ready to become tainted. The women put it into some pool or stagnant water for the space of two or three months, at the end of which time they take it out, and it is used for feasts of great importance, cooked like *Neintahouy*. They also eat it baked under hot ashes, licking their fingers as they handle these stinking ears, just as if they were sugar-cane, although the taste and smell are very strong, and the stink worse even than sewers. This corn made rotten in such a way was no food for me, however they might relish it, nor did I willingly touch it with my fingers or my hand because of the bad smell it gave and left on them for several days. So they did not offer it to me any more when they had perceived my disgust at it. They also make a dish with acorns, which they boil in several waters to take away the bitter taste, and I found them quite good. They also sometimes eat raw a sort of tree-bark, like willow-bark, and I have eaten it to be like the savages. But herbs they do not eat at all, neither cooked nor raw, except certain roots they call *Sondhratatte* and others similar to them.

Before the arrival of the French in the country of the Canadians and the other nomad tribes their entire household material was only of wood, bark, or stone. Of the stone they made axes and knives, and of wood and bark they made all their other utensils and household furniture, even kettles, buckets, or troughs for cooking their meat, which they cooked or rather made tender in the following manner. They heated a quantity of stones and gravel red-hot in a good fire, then they threw them into a kettle filled with water in which was the meat or the fish to be cooked, and whenever they took these out they put in others in their place, and in course of time the water was heated and so cooked the meat to some extent. But the Hurons and other sedentary tribes and nations used and knew how to make earthenware pots, as they still do, firing them in their ovens. These are very good and do not break when set on the fire even though they may not have water in them. But they cannot stand moisture and cold water for long, but become soft and break at the least blow given them; otherwise they last for a very long time. The women savages make them, taking suitable earth which they sift and pulverize very thoroughly, mixing with it a little sandstone. Then when the lump has been shaped like a ball they put a hole in it with their fist, and this they keep enlarging, scraping it inside with a little wooden paddle as much and as long as is necessary to complete the work. These pots are made without feet and without handles, quite round like a ball, except for the mouth which projects a little.

John Lawson, A New Voyage to Carolina (*Richmond*, 1937), *pp*. 219-223.

When these Savages go a hunting, they commonly go out in great Numbers, and oftentimes a great many Days' Journey from home, beginning at the coming in of the Winter; that is, when the Leaves are fallen from the Trees and are become dry. Tis then they burn the Woods by setting Fire to the Leaves and withered Bent and Grass, which they do with a Match made of the black Moss that hangs on the Trees in Carolina, and is sometimes above six Foot long. This, when dead, becomes black, (though of an Ash-Colour) and will then hold Fire as well as the best Match we have in Europe. In Places where this Moss is not found, (as towards the Mountains) they make Lintels of the Bark of cypress beaten, which serve as well. Thus they go and fire the Woods for many Miles, and drive the Deer and other Game into small Necks of Land and Isthmuses where they kill and destroy what they please. In these Hunting-Quarters they have their Wives and Ladies of the Camp, where they eat all the Fruits and Dainties of that Country, and live in all the Mirth and Jollity which it is possible for such People to entertain themselves withal. Here it is that they get their Complement of Deer-Skins and Furs to trade with the English, (the Deer-Skins being in Season in Winter which is contrary to England.) All small Game, as Turkies, Ducks and small Vermine, they commonly kill with Bow and Arrow, thinking it not worth throwing Powder and Shot after them. Of Turkies they have abundance, especially in Oak-Land, as most of it is that lies any distance backwards. I have been often in their Hunting-Quarters where a roasted or barbakued Turkey, eaten with Bear's Fat, is held a good Dish, and indeed I approve of it very well; for the Bear's Grease is the sweetest and less offensive to the Stomach, (as I said before) of any Fat of Animals I ever tasted. The Savage Men never beat their Corn to make Bread; but that is the Women's Work, especially the Girls, of whom you shall see four beating with long great Pestils in a narrow wooden Mortar; and every one keeps her Stroke so exactly, that tis worthy of Admiration. Their Cookery continues from Morning till Night. The Hunting makes them hungry, and the Indians are a People that always eat very often, not seldom getting up at Midnight to eat. They plant a great many sorts of Pulse, Part of which they eat green in the Summer, keeping great Quantities for their Winter-Store, which they carry along with them into the Hunting-Quarters and eat them.

The small red Pease is very common with them, and they eat a great deal of that and other sorts boiled with their Meat, or eaten with Bear's Fat, which Food makes them break Wind backwards, which the Men frequently do and laugh heartily at it, it being accounted no ill Manners amongst the Indians; Yet the Women are more modest than to follow that ill Custom. At their setting out, they have Indians to attend their Hunting Camp that are not good and expert Hunters; therefore are employed to carry Burdens, to get Bark for the Cabins, and other Servile Work; also to go backward and forward to their Towns, to carry News to the old People, whom they leave behind them. The Women are forced to carry their Loads of Grain and other Provisions and get Fire-Wood; for a good Hunter or Warriour in these Expeditions, is employed in no other Business than the Affairs of Game and Battle. The wild Fruits which are dried in the Summer, over Fires, on Hurdles and in the Sun, are now brought into the Field; as are likewise the Cakes and Quiddonies of Peaches

and that Fruit and Bilberries dried, of which, they stew and make
Fruit-Bread and Cakes. In some parts where Pigeons are plentiful,
they get of their Fat enough to supply their Winter Stores. Thus they
abide in these Quarters all the Winter long, till the Time approach for
planting their Maiz and other Fruits. In these quarters, at Spare-
hours, the Women make Baskets and Mats to lie upon, and those
that are not extraordinary Hunters, make Bowls, Dishes and Spoons,
of Gum-wood, and the Tulip-Tree, others (where they find a Vein of
white Clay, fit for their purpose) make Tobacco-pipes, all which are
often transported to other Indians, that perhaps have greater Plenty
of Deer and other Game; so they buy, with these Manufactures, their
raw Skins, with the Hair on, which our neighboring Indians bring to
their Towns, and in the Summertime, make the Slaves and sorry
Hunters dress them, the Winter-Sun being not strong enough to dry
them; and those that are dried in the Cabins are black and nasty with
the Light-Wood Smoke, which they commonly burn. Their way of
Dressing their Skins is, by soaking them in Water, so they get the
Hair off with an Instrument made of the Bone of a Deer's Foot; yet
some use a sort of Iron Drawing-Knife, which they purchase of the
English, and after the Hair is off they dissolve Deer's Brains, (which
before hand are made in a Cake and baked in the Embers) in a Bowl
of Water, so soak the Skins therein till the Brains have sucked up the
Water; then they dry it gently, and keep working it with an Oyster-
Shell, or some such thing, to scrape withal till it is dry; whereby it
becomes soft and pliable. Yet these so dressed will not endure wet,
but become hard thereby; which to prevent, they either cure them in
the Smoke or tan them with Bark, as before observed; not but that
young Indian Corn beaten to a Pulp, will effect the same as the
Brains. They are not only good Hunters of the wild Beasts and Game
of the Forest, but very expert in taking the Fish of the Rivers and
Waters near which they inhabit, and are acquainted withal. Thus
they that live a great way up the Rivers practice Striking Sturgeon
and Rockfish, or Bass, when they come up the Rivers to spawn;
besides the vast Shoals of Sturgeon which they kill and take with
Snares, as we do Pike in Europe. The Herrings, in March and April,
run a great way up the Rivers and fresh Streams to spawn, where the
Savages make great Wares with Hedges that hinder their Passage
only in the Middle, where an artificial Pound is made to take them

in, so that they cannot return. This Method is in use all over the Fresh Streams, to catch Trout and the other Species of Fish which those Parts afford. Their taking of Crawfish is so pleasant, that I cannot pass it by without mention; When they have a mind to get these Shell-fish, they take a Piece of Venison and half barbakue or roast it, then they cut it into thin Slices, which Slices they stick through with Reeds about six Inches asunder betwixt Piece and Piece; then the Reeds are made sharp at one end; and so they stick a great many of them down in the bottom of the Water, (thus baited) in the small Brooks and Runs, which the Craw-fish frequent. Thus the Indians sit by and tend those baited Sticks, every now and then taking them up to see how many are at the Bait; where they generally find abundance, so take them off and put them in a Basket for the Purpose, and stick the Reeds down again. By this Method, they will, in a little time, catch several Bushels, which are as good as any I ever eat. Those Indians that frequent the Salt-Waters, take abundance of Fish, some very large and of several sorts, which to preserve, they first barbakue, then pull the Fish to Pieces, so dry it in the Sun, whereby it keeps for Transportation; as for Scate, Oysters, Cockles, and several sorts of Shell-fish, they open and dry them upon Hurdles, having a constant Fire under them. The Hurdles are made of Reeds of Canes in the shape of a Gridiron. Thus they dry several Bushels of these Fish and keep them for their Necessities. At the time when they are on the Salts, and Sea-Coasts, they have another Fishery, that is for a little Shell-Fish, which those in England call Blackmoors Teeth. These they catch by tying Bits of Oysters to a long String, which they lay in such Places, as they know, those Shell-Fish haunt. These Fish get hold of the Oysters, and suck them in, so that they pull up those long Strings, and take great Quantities of them, which they carry a great way into the main Land, to trade with the remote Indians, where they are of great Value; but never near the Sea, by reason they are common, therefore not esteemed. Besides, the Youth and Indian Boys go in the Night, and one holding a Light-Wood Torch, the other has a Bow and Arrows, and the Fire directing him to see the Fish, he shoots them with the Arrows; and thus they kill a great many of the smaller Fry, and sometimes pretty large ones. It is an established Custom amongst all these Natives, that the young Hunter never eats of that Buck, Bear, Fish, or any other Game, which happens to be the first they kill of that sort; because they believe, if he should eat thereof, he would never after be fortunate in Hunting. The like foolish Ceremony they hold, when they have made a Ware to take Fish withal; if a big bellied Woman eat of the first Dish that is caught in it, they say, that Ware will never take much Fish; and as for killing of Snakes, they avoid it, if they lie in their way, because their Opinion is, that some of the Serpents Kindred would kill some of the Savages' Relations, that should destroy him. They have thousands of these foolish Ceremonies and Beliefs, which they are strict Observers of.

Mary Jemison was born in 1743 aboard the ship that took her parents from Ireland to Philadelphia. In 1755, her family was captured and killed by French-allied Indians and she was adopted into the Seneca tribe. She married a Delaware, bore him several children, and, despite several opportunities to return to white society, remained with the Indians the rest of her life. She told her story to James Seaver before she died, and in 1824, he published it as A Narrative of the Life of Mary Jemison. *The following excerpt is from the 7th edition (New York) of 1910, pp. 69-72.*

I had then been with the Indians four summers and four winters, and had become so far accustomed to their mode of living, habits, and dispositions, that my anxiety to get away, to be set at liberty and leave them, had almost subsided. With them was my home; my family was there, and there I had many friends to whom I was warmly attached in consideration of the favors, affection, and friendship with which they had uniformily treated me from the time of my adoption. Our labor was not severe; and that of one year was exactly similar in almost every respect to that of the others, without that endless variety that is to be observed in the common labor of the white people. Notwithstanding the Indian women have all the fuel and bread to procure, and the cooking to perform, their task is probably not harder than that of white women, who have those articles provided for them; and their cares certainly are not half as numerous, nor as great. In the summer season, we planted, tended, and harvested our corn, and generally had all our children with us;

but had no master to oversee or drive us, so that we could work as leisurely as we pleased. We had no plows on the Ohio, but performed the whole process of planting and hoeing with a small tool that resembled, in some respects, a hoe with a very short handle.

We pursued our farming business according to the general custom of Indian women, which is as follows: In order to expedite their business, and at the same time enjoy each other's company, they all work together in one field, or at whatever job they may have on hand. In the spring, they choose an old active squaw to be their driver and overseer, when at labor, for the ensuing year. She accepts the honor, and they consider themselves bound to obey her.

When the time for planting arrives, and the soil is prepared, the squaws are assembled in the morning, and conducted into a field, where each plants one row. They then go into the next field and plant once across, and so on till they have gone through the tribe. If any remains to be planted, they again commence where they did at first, (in the same field,) and so keep on till the whole is finished. By this rule, they perform their labor of every kind, and every jealousy of one having done more or less than another is effectually avoided.

Each squaw cuts her own wood; but it is all brought to the house under the direction of the overseer. . .

Our cooking consisted in pounding our corn into samp or hominy, boiling the hominy, making now and then a cake and baking it in the ashes, and in boiling or roasting our venison. As our cooking and eating utensils consisted of a hominy block and pestle, a small kettle, a knife or two, and a few vessels of bark or wood, it required but little time to keep them in order for use.

Spinning, weaving, sewing, stocking knitting, and the like, are arts which have never been practiced in the Indian tribes generally. After the revolutionary war, I learned to sew, so that I could make my own clothing after a poor fashion; but I have been wholly ignorant of the application of the other domestic arts since my captivity. In the season of hunting, it was our business, in addition to our cooking, to bring home the game that was taken by the Indians, dress it, and carefully preserve the eatable meat, and prepare or dress the skins.

John Long, Voyages and Travels of an Indian Interpreter and Trader, *ed. Milo Milton Quaife (Chicago, 1922), pp. 68-70.*

Indians in general are extremely indolent, from the wildest to the most civilized, and value themselves upon being so, conceiving it beneath the dignity of a warrior to labor, and that all domestic cares and concerns are the province of women alone. This aversion for labor does not arise from dread, or dislike of fatigue; on the contrary, no people encounter or endure it with more cheerfulness, particularly in their amusements, which are of various kinds, and many of them violent and laborious. They are calculated to make them athletic, and at the same time by the profuse perspiration which they occasion, they render the joints supple, and enable them to hunt with more facility.

Playing at ball, which is a favorite game, is very fatiguing. The ball is about the size of a cricket ball, made of deer skin and stuffed with hair; this is driven forwards and backwards with short sticks, about two feet long, and broad at the end like a bat, worked like a racket, but with larger interstices. By this the ball is impelled, and from the elasticity of the racket, which is composed of deer's sinews, is thrown to a great distance. The game is played by two parties, and the contest lies in intercepting each other, and striking the ball into a goal, at the distance of about four hundred yards, at the extremity of which are placed two high poles, about the width of a wicket from each other. The victory consists in driving the ball between the poles. The Indians play with great good humor and even when one of them happens, in the heat of the game, to strike another with his stick, it is not resented. But these accidents are cautiously avoided, as the violence with which they strike has been known to break an arm or a leg.

Athtergain, or miss-none-but-catch-all, is also a favorite amusement with them, in which the women frequently take a part. It is played with a number of hard beans, black and white, one of which has small spots and is called the king. They are put into a shallow wooden bowl, and shaken alternately by each party, who sit on the ground opposite to one another; whoever is dexterous enough to make the spotted bean jump out of the bowl, receives of the adverse party as many beans as there are spots. The rest of the beans do not count for anything.

The boys are very expert at trundling a hoop, particularly the Cahnuaga Indians, whom I have frequently seen excel at this amusement. The game is played by any number of boys who may accidentally assemble together, some driving the hoop, while others with bows and arrows shoot at it. At this exercise they are surprisingly expert, and will stop the progress of the hoop when going with great velocity, by driving the pointed arrow into its edge; this they will do at a considerable distance, and on horseback as well as on foot. They will also kill small birds at fifty yards' distance, and strike a half-penny off a stick at fifteen yards. Spears and tomahawks they manage with equal dexterity.

James Adair, History of the American Indians, *ed. Samuel Cole Williams (Johnson City, Tenn., 1930), pp. 428-431.*

The Indians are much addicted to gaming, and will often stake every thing they possess. Ball-playing is their chief and most favourite game: and is such severe exercise, as to shew it was originally calculated for a hardy and expert race of people, like themselves, and the ancient Spartans. The ball is made of a piece of scraped deer-skin, moistened, and stuffed hard with deer's hair, and strongly sewed with deer's sinews.—The ball-sticks are about two feet long, the lower end somewhat resembling the palm of a hand, and which are worked with deer-skin thongs. Between these, they catch the ball, and throw it a great distance, when not prevented by some of the opposite party, who fly to intercept them. The goal is about five hundred yards in length: at each end of it, they fix two long bending poles into the ground, three yards apart below, but slanting a considerable way outwards. The party that happens to throw the ball over these, counts one; but, if it be thrown underneath, it is cast back, and played for as usual. The gamesters are equal in number on each side; and, at the beginning of every course of the ball, they throw it up high in the center of the ground, and in a direct line between the two goals. When the crowd of players prevents the one who catched the ball, from throwing it off with a long direction, he commonly sends it the right course, by an artful sharp twirl. They are so exceedingly expert in this manly exercise, that, between the goals, the ball is mostly flying the different ways, by the force of the playing sticks, without falling to the ground, for they are not allowed to catch it with their hands. It is surprising to see how swiftly they fly, when closely chased by a nimble footed pursuer; when they are intercepted by one of the opposite party, his fear of being cut by the ball sticks, commonly gives them an opportunity of throwing it perhaps a hundred yards; but the antagonist sometimes runs up behind, and by a sudden stroke dashes down the ball. It is a very unusual thing to see them act spitefully in any sort of game, not even in this severe and tempting exercise.

Once, indeed, I saw some break the legs and arms of their opponents, by hurling them down, when on a descent, and running at full speed. But I afterward understood, there was a family dispute of long continuance between them: that might have raised their spleen, as much as the high bets they had then at stake, which was almost all they were worth. The Choktah are exceedingly addicted to gaming, and frequently on the slightest and most hazardous occasion, will lay their all, and as much as their credit can procure.

By education, precept, and custom, as well as strong example, they have learned to shew an external acquiescence in every thing that befalls them, either as to life or death. By this means, they reckon it a scandal to the character of a steady warrior to let his temper be ruffled by any accidents,—their virtue they say, should prevent it. Their conduct is equal to their belief of the power of those principles: previous to this sharp exercise of ball playing, notwithstanding the irreligion of the Choktah in other respects, they will supplicate *Yo He Wah*, to bless them with success. To move the deity to enable them to conquer the party they are to play against, they mortify themselves in a surprising manner; and, except a small intermission, their female relations dance out of doors all the preceding night, chanting religious notes with their shrill voices, to move *Yo He Wah* to be favourable to their kindred party on the morrow. The men fast and wake from sunset, till the ball play is over the next day, which is about one or two o'clock in the afternoon. During the whole night, they are to forbear sleeping under the penalty of reproaches and shame; which would sit very sharp upon them, if their party chanced to lose the game, as it would be ascribed to that unmanly and vicious conduct. They turn out to the ball ground, in a long row, painted white, whooping, as if Pluto's prisoners were all broke loose: when that enthusiastic emotion is over, the leader of the company begins a religious invocation, by saying *Yah*, short; then *Yo* long, which the rest of the train repeat with a short accent, and on a low key like the leader: and thus they proceed with such acclamations and invocations, as have been already noticed, on other occasions. Each party are desirous to gain the twentieth ball, which they esteem a favourite divine gift. As it is in the time of laying by the corn, in the very heat of summer, they use this severe exercise, a stranger would wonder to see them hold it so long at full speed, and under the scorching sun, hungry also, and faint with the excessive use of such sharp physic as the button snake root, the want of natural rest, and of every kind of nourishment. But their constancy, which they gain by custom, and their love of virtue, as the sure means of success, enable them to perform all their exercises, without failing in the least, be they ever so severe in the pursuit.

The warriors have another favourite game, called *Chungke*; which, with propriety of language, may be called "Running hard labour." They have near their state house, a square piece of ground well cleaned, and fine sand is carefully strewed over it, when requisite, to promote a swifter motion to what they throw along the surface. Only one, or two on a side, play at this ancient game. They have a stone about two fingers broad at the edge, and two spans round: each party has a pole of about eight feet long, smooth, and tapering at each end, the points flat. They set off a-breast of each other at six yards from the end of the play ground; then one of them hurls the stone on its edge, in as direct a line as he can, a considerable distance toward the middle of the other end of the square: when they have ran a few yards, each darts his pole anointed with bear's oil, with a proper force, as near as he can guess in proportion to the motion of the stone, that the end may lie close to the stone—when this is the case, the person counts two of the game, and, in proportion to the nearness of the poles to the mark, one is counted, unless by measuring, both are found to be at an equal distance from the stone. In this manner, the players will keep running most part of the day, at half speed, under the violent heat of the sun, staking their silver ornaments, their nose, finger, and ear rings; their breast, arm, and wrist plates, and even all their wearing apparel, except that which barely covers their middle. All the American Indians are much addicted to this game, which to us appears to be a task of stupid drudgery: it seems however to be of early origin, when their fore-fathers used diversions as simple as their manners. The hurling stones they use at present, were time immemorial rubbed smooth on the rocks, and with prodigious labour; they are kept with the strictest religious care, from one generation to another, and are exempted from being buried with the dead. They belong to the town where they are used, and are carefully preserved.

V. RIGHT AND WRONG

Every society has rules, written or unwritten, and means of enforcing them which seek to impose some degree of order upon the behavior of its members. Since the Indians had no writing, how were their laws made known? How were they enforced? Was there any mercy in Indian law? Was Indian government similar to a European monarchy? How were its leaders chosen? What were their duties? Why did an Indian obey his leaders? Did the Indians have a police force to compel obedience? What was the chief form of punishment? How did they provide for the social welfare of the orphaned, the poor, the sick, and the aged? Were old people respected? Why? Did the Indians hold land privately? Was this a source of social conflict? What role did revenge play in Indian life? Was it, according to Indian culture, "right" or "wrong"? How did the European observers regard Indian law? Did they find it inferior or superior to European law?

Chrestien Le Clercq, New Relation of Gaspesia, *ed. William F. Ganong (Toronto, 1910), pp. 234-239.*

It is certain that laws have been the foundation of the most flourishing monarchies of the world. This is why they are called, and rightly, the soul of the republics, of the kingdoms, and of the empires of the universe, because these survive only in proportion as their peoples faithfully obey their laws. Consequently one cannot, it seems to me, give to-day a more convincing reason for the decadence of the Gaspesian nation, formerly one of the most numerous and most flourishing of Canada, than their disregard for the fundamental laws which the elders had established, but which our Indians have not observed, and still do not observe at present, except in so far as it pleases them; for it is truth to say that they have neither faith, nor king, nor laws. One sees no more among these people those large assemblies in the form of councils, nor that supreme authority of the heads of families, elders, and chiefs, who regulated civil and criminal affairs, and in the last resort decided upon war and upon peace, giving such orders as they thought absolutely essential, and enforcing the observance thereof with much submission and fidelity. There are now only two or three Indians who, in their own districts still preserve, though feebly, a sort of power and authority, if one can say that such is found among these peoples. The most prominent chief is followed by several young warriors and by several hunters, who act always as his escort, and who fall in under arms when this ruler wishes particular distinction upon some special occasion. But, in fact, all his power and authority are based only upon the good will of those of his nation, who execute his orders just in so far as it pleases them. We had among us, at the River of Saint Joseph, one of these old chiefs whom our Gaspesians considered as their head and their ruler, much more because of his family, which was very numerous, than because of his sovereign power, of which they have shaken off the yoke, and which they are not willing any longer to recognise.

The occupation of this chief was to assign the places for hunting, and to take the furs of the Indians, giving them in return whatever they needed. This man made it a point of honour to be always the worst dressed of his people, and to take care that they all were better clothed than he. He held it as a maxim, as he told me one day, that a ruler, and a great heart like his, ought to take more care for others than for himself, because, good hunter as he was, he always obtained easily everything which he needed for his own use, and that as for the rest, if he did not himself live well, he should find his desire in the affection and the hearts of his subjects. It was as if he had wished to say that his treasures and riches were in the hearts and in the affection of his people.

It happened that a stranger wished to dispute his right of command, or at least to share with this ruler that government, with its imaginary grandeur, for which he had as much regard as if it were the greatest empire of the world. This competitor arrived well provided with axes, with guns, with blankets, with beavers, and with everything which could give him some prominence and some entrance into the sovereignty which he claimed was properly due him by right of hereditary succession, because his father had been formerly head and chief of the Gaspesian nation. "Very well," said our Indian, "show that thy heart is a true chief's heart and worthy of absolute empire over the people whom I rule. There," continued he, "are some poor Indians who are wholly naked; give them thy robes of otter and beaver. Thou seest, again, that I am the worst dressed of all, and it is through this that I wish to appear chief—through despoiling and depriving myself of everything in order to aid my Indians. Therefore, when following my example, thou shouldst be as poor as I. Let us go a-hunting when the time is right, and the one of us who kills the most moose and beavers shall be the legitimate king of all the Gaspesians." The stranger accepted this challenge with spirit. In imitation of our chief, he gave away everything he had, and kept back nothing except the bare necessaries. He went hunting, but he was so unfortunate as to do it very badly, and consequently he was obliged to abandon the enterprise which he had formed of commanding our Gaspesians, who did not wish to recognise any other head than their old and brave chief whom they obeyed with pleasure.

The Gaspesians have at present no fundamental laws which serve them as regulations. They make up and end all their quarrels and their differences through friends and through arbiters. If it is, however, a question of punishing a criminal who has killed or assassinated some Indian, he is condemned to death without other form of law. "Take care, my friend," say they, "if thou killest, thou shalt be killed." This is often carried out by command of the elders, who assemble in council upon the subject, and often by the private authority of individuals, without any trial of the case being made, provided that it is evident the criminal has deserved death.

Neither prisons, racks, wheels, nor gibbets are in use among these people, as in Europe. All are satisfied if the head of the guilty person is broken with a blow of an axe or a club. The other tortures are kept solely for tormenting and killing prisoners of war.

It is the right of the head of the nation, according to the customs of the country, which serve as laws and regulations to the Gaspesians, to distribute the places of hunting to each individual. It is not permitted to any Indian to overstep the bounds and limits of the region which shall have been assigned him in the assemblies of the elders. These are held in autumn and spring expressly to make this assignment.

The young people must strictly obey the orders of the chiefs. When it is a question of going to war, they must allow themselves to be led, and must attack and fight the nation which they wish to destroy, in the manner which has been planned by the head of their council of war.

It is not permissible for any Indian to marry his relative. One never sees among our Gaspesians those incestuous marriages of father with daughter, of son with mother, of sister with brother, of uncle with niece, nor even of cousin with cousin. Incest is held in horror among them, and they have always testified to much aversion for this crime.

The one of our Indians who wishes to marry a girl must live an entire year in the wigwam of his mistress's father, whom he must serve and to whom he must give all the furs of moose and beavers which he kills in hunting. By the same law it is forbidden to the future husband and wife to abandon themselves to their pleasure.

After the death of one's brother, it is permissible to marry his wife, in order that she may have children of the same blood if she has not had any by her first husband.

If, when the father of a family is dead, the widow contracts a second marriage, it is necessary that the eldest son take the care of his brothers and sisters, and that he build a separate wigwam. This is for the purpose of avoiding bad treatment by their step-father, and in order not to cause any trouble in the housekeeping.

It is the duty of the head man and chief to have care over the orphans. The chiefs are obliged to distribute them among the wigwams of the best hunters, in order that they may be supported and brought up as if they were the own children of the latter.

All the Gaspesians must without fail aid the sick; and those who have meat or fish in abundance must give some of it to those who are in need.

It is a crime among our Indians not to be hospitable. They receive all strangers who are not their enemies very kindly into their wigwams.

They must take great care of the bones of the dead, and must bury everything which was in use by the deceased, in order that the spirits of each thing, such as his snowshoes, guns, axes, kettles, &c., may render him service in the Land of Souls.

According to the Gaspesian laws, it is allowable to break marriages and declare them void when those who are married have no longer any affection for one another.

It is considered shameful to show anger or impatience for the insults that are offered, or the misfortunes which come, to the Indians, at least unless this is to defend the honour and reputation of the dead, who cannot, say they, avenge themselves, nor obtain satisfaction for the insults and affronts which are done them.

It is forbidden them by the laws and customs of the country to pardon or to forgive any one of their enemies, unless great presents are given on behalf of these to the whole nation, or to those who have been injured.

The women have no command among the Indians. They must needs obey the orders of their husbands. They have no rights in the councils, nor in the public feasts. It is the same, as to this, with the young men who have not yet killed any moose, the death of which opens the portal to the honours of the Gaspesian nation, and gives to the young men the right to assist at public and private assemblies. One is always a young man, that is to say, one has no more rights than the children, the women, and the girls, as long as he has not killed a moose.

Adriaen Van der Donck, A Description of the New Netherlands, *ed. Thomas F. O'Donnell (Syracuse, 1968), pp. 100-101.*

The common rules of order in the administration of justice are not observed among this people, and are not exercised to protect the innocent or to punish the guilty. There is so little order observed among them that the Netherlanders, who reside there and traffic with them, are astonished to find that such societies can remain united, where there is no regard paid to the administration of justice. All minor offences, such as stealing, adultery, lying, cheating, and the like wrongs against civil order, pass unpunished among them. I have known that an unmarried woman murdered her own child, and although the fact was well known, still she went unpunished; and also that an Indian, on several occasions, violated several women whom he found alone in the woods and in lonely places, who also passed unpunished. With those exceptions, during a residence of nine years in the country, I have not heard of any capital offences. Stealing is quite common among them, but not of articles of great value. It may be a knife, an axe, a pair of shoes, a pair of stockings, or such like articles. When we detect them with the goods, we may retake the same and chastise them freely; and when the thief is not known and the matter is represented to the chief, the property is usually restored. On those occasions the thief is reprimanded by the chief for his conduct, and although reproof is the highest punishment suffered by the culprit, yet it will not readily show how much they fear such treatment, and how uncommon crimes are among them. With us a watchful police is supported, and crimes are more frequent than among them.

Murder or personal injuries are not attended to by the chief, or friends, except for the purpose of reconciling the parties, for which they use all possible means, and give liberally to effect their object when the offender is deficient in means, which is usually the case. A murder among them is never atoned for without heavy payment. The nearest relative by blood always is the avenger, and if he finds the murderer within twenty-four hours after the act, he is slain instantly, but if the murderer can save himself until one day is past, and the avenger slays him afterwards, then he is liable to be pursued and slain in like manner. A murderer seldom is killed after the first twenty-four hours are past, but he must flee and remain concealed; when the friends endeavour to reconcile the parties, which is frequently agreed to, on condition that the nearest relatives of the murderer, be they men, women, or children, on meeting the relatives of the person murdered, must give way to them.

Persons are very seldom doomed to death among them, except captives taken in war, whom they consider to have forfeited the rights of man. Such they condemn to be burned. This they usually do slowly, beginning with their hands and feet. The torture sometimes lasts three days before the victim expires, who continues to sing and dance until life is extinct, reproaching his tormentors, deriding their conduct, and extolling the bravery of his own nation.

Robert Beverley, The History and Present State of Virginia, *ed. David Freeman Hawke (Indianapolis, 1971), pp. 114-116.*

The Indians having no sort of letters among them, as has been before observed, they can have no written laws. Nor did the constitution in which we found them seem to need many, nature and their own convenience having taught them to obey one chief who is arbiter of all things among them. They claim no property in lands, but they are in common to a whole nation. Everyone hunts and fishes and gathers fruits in all places. Their labor in tending corn, pompions, melons, etc., is not so great that they need quarrel for room where the land is so fertile and where so much lies uncultivated.

They bred no sort of cattle nor had anything that could be called riches. They valued skins and furs for use and peak and roanoke for ornament.

They are very severe in punishing ill breeding, of which every werowance is undisputed judge, who never fails to lay a rigorous penalty upon it. An example whereof I had from a gentleman that was an eye witness, which was this:

In the time of Bacon's Rebellion, one of these werowances, attended by several others of his nation, was treating with the English in New Kent County about a peace. And during the time of his speech one of his attendants presumed to interrupt him, which he resented as the most unpardonable affront that could be offered him; and therefore he instantly took his tomahawk from his girdle and split the fellow's head for his presumption. The poor fellow dying immediately upon the spot, he commanded some of his men to carry him out and went on again with his speech where he left off as unconcerned as if nothing had happened.

The Indians never forget nor forgive an injury till satisfaction be given, be it national or personal. But it becomes the business of their whole lives, and even after that the revenge is entailed upon their posterity till full reparation be made.

The titles of honor that I have observed among them peculiar to themselves are only cockarouse and werowance besides that of the king and queen. But of late they have borrowed some titles from us which they bestow among themselves. A cockarouse is one that has the honor to be of the king or queen's council with relation to the affairs of the government and has a great share in the administration. A werowance is a military officer who, of course, takes upon him the command of all parties either of hunting, traveling, warring, or the like, and the word signifies a war captain.

The priests and conjurers are also of great authority; the people having recourse to them for counsel and direction upon all occasions, by which means and by help of the first fruits and frequent offerings they riot in the fat of the land and grow rich upon the spoils of their ignorant countrymen.

They have also people of a rank inferior to the commons, a sort of servants among them. These are called black boys and are attendant upon the gentry to do their servile offices, which in their seat of nature are not many. For they live barely up to the present relief of their necessities and make all things easy and comfortable to themselves by the indulgence of a kind climate without toiling and perplexing their mind for riches, which other people often trouble themselves to provide for uncertain and ungrateful heirs. In short, they seem as possessing nothing and yet enjoying all things.

John Heckewelder, An Account of the History, Manners, and Customs, of the Indian Nations, who once Inhabited Pennsylvania and the Neighbouring States, *in* Transactions of the American Philosophical Society, *volume 1 (1819), pp. 152-155.*

There is no nation in the world who pay greater respect to old age than the American Indians. From their infancy they are taught to be kind and attentive to aged persons, and never to let them suffer for want of necessaries or comforts. The parents spare no pains to impress upon the minds of their children the conviction that they would draw down upon themselves the anger of the Great Spirit, were they to neglect those whom, in his goodness, he had permitted to attain such an advanced age, whom he had protected with his almighty power through all the perils and dangers of life, while so many had perished by wars, accidents and sickness in various forms, by the incantations of the wizzard or the stroke of the murderer, and not a few by the consequences of their own imprudent conduct.

It is a sacred principle among the Indians, and one of those moral and religious truths which they have always before their eyes, that the Great Spirit who created them, and provided them so abundantly with the means of subsistence, made it the duty of parents to maintain and take care of their children until they should be able to provide for themselves, and that having while weak and helpless received the benefits of maintenance, education and protection, they are bound to repay them by a similar care of those who are labouring under the infirmities of old age, and are no longer able to supply their own wants.

Thus, a strong feeling of gratitude towards their elders, inculcated and cherished from their earliest infancy, is the solid foundation on which rests that respect for old age for which Indians are so remarkable, and it is further supported by the well-founded hope of receiving the like succours and attentions in their turn, when the heavy hand of time shall have reduced them to the same helpless situation which they now commiserate in others, and seek by every means in their power to render more tolerable. Hence, they do not confine themselves to acts of absolute necessity; it is not enough for them that the old are not suffered to starve with hunger or perish with cold, but they must be made as much as possible to share in the pleasures and comforts of life. It is, indeed, a moving spectacle to see the tender and delicate attentions which, on every occasion, they lavish upon aged and decrepid persons. When going out a hunting they will put them on a horse or in a canoe, and take them into the woods to their hunting ground, in order to revive their spirits by making them enjoy the sight of a sport in which they can no longer participate. They place them in particular situations, where they are sure that the game they are in pursuit of will pass by, taking proper measures at the same time to prevent its escape, so that their aged parents and friends may, at least, as our sportsmen call it, *be in at the death*. Nor is this all; the hoary veterans must also enjoy the honours of the chase; when the animal, thus surrounded, is come within reach of their guns, when every possibility of escape is precluded, by the woods all around being set on fire, they all, young and old, fire together, so that it is difficult to decide whose ball it was that brought the animal to the ground. But they never are at a loss to decide, and always give it in favour of the oldest man in the party. So, when the young people have discovered a place where the bears have their haunts, or have resorted to for the winter, they frequently take with them to the spot, such of the old men as are yet able to walk or ride, where they not only have an opportunity of witnessing the sport, but receive their full share of the meat and oil.

At home the old are as well treated and taken care of as if they were favourite children. They are cherished and even caressed; indulged in health and nursed in sickness; and all their wishes and wants are anticipated. Their company is sought by the young, to whom their conversation is considered an honour. Their advice is asked on all occasions, their words are listened to as oracles, and their occasional garrulity, nay, even the second childhood often attendant on extreme old age, is never with Indians a subject of ridicule, or laughter. Respect, gratitude and love are too predominant in their minds to permit any degrading idea to mix itself with these truly honourable and generous feelings.

On every occasion, and in every situation through life, age takes the lead among the Indians. Even little boys, when going on parties of pleasure, were it only to catch butterflies, strictly adhere to this rule, and submit to the direction of the oldest in their company, who is their chief, leader and spokesman; if they are accosted on the way by any person, and asked whither they are going, or any other question, no one will presume to answer but their *speaker*. The same rule is observed when they are grown up, and in no case whatever will one of a party, club or meeting, attempt to assume authority over the leader, or even to set him right if he should mistake the road or take a wrong course; much less will any one contradict what he says, unless his opinion should be particularly asked, in which case, and no other, he will give his advice, but with great modesty and diffidence.

And yet there have been travellers who have ventured to assert that old people among the Indians are not only neglected and suffered to perish for want, but that they are even, when no longer able to take care of themselves, *put out of the way of all trouble*. I am free to declare, that among all the Indian nations that I have become acquainted with, if any one should kill an old man or woman for no other cause than that of having become useless or burdensome to society, it would be considered as an unpardonable crime, the general indignation would be excited, and the murderer instantly put to death. I cannot conceive any act that would produce such an universal horror and detestation, such is the veneration which is every where felt for old age.

James Smith was born in 1737 on the frontier of Pennsylvania where he was captured by Indians at the age of eighteen. He was adopted into their tribe and for four years shared their life until his escape in 1759. He later served in the British forces against the Indians and still later against the British in the Revolution. An Account of the Remarkable Occurrences in the Life and Travels of Col. James Smith during his Captivity with the Indians, in the Years 1755, '56, '57, '58, & '59 *was published in Lexington Kentucky, in 1799. The following passage is taken from the reprint in the* Ohio Valley Historical Series, *number 5 (1907), pp. 149-151.*

I have often heard of Indian Kings, but never saw any.—How any term used by the Indians in their own tongue, for the chief man of a nation, could be rendered King, I know not. The chief of a nation is neither a supreme ruler, monarch or potentate—He can neither make war or peace, leagues or treaties—He cannot impress soldiers, or dispose of magazines—He cannot adjourn, prorogue or dissolve a general assembly, nor can he refuse his assent to their conclusions, or in any manner controul them—With them there is no such thing as heriditary succession, title of nobility or royal blood, even talked of—The chief of a nation, even with the consent of his assembly, or council, cannot raise one shilling of tax off the citizens, but only receive what they please to give as free and voluntary donations.—The chief of a nation has to hunt for his living, as any other citizen—How then can they with any propriety, be called kings? I apprehend that the white people were formerly so fond of the name of kings, and so ignorant of their power, that they concluded the chief man of a nation must be a king.

As they are illiterate, they consequently have no written code of laws. What they execute as laws, are either old customs, or the immediate result of new councils. Some of their ancient laws or customs are very pernicious, and disturb the public weal. Their vague law of marriage is a glaring instance of this, as the man and his wife are under no legal obligation to live together, if they are both willing to part. They have little form, or ceremony among them, in matrimony, but do like the Israelites of old—the man goes in unto the woman, and she becomes his wife. The years of puberty and the age of consent, is about fourteen for the women, and eighteen for the men. Before I was taken by the Indians, I had often heard that in the ceremony of marriage, the man gave the woman a deer's leg, and she gave him a red ear of corn, signifying that she was to keep him in bread, and he was to keep her in meat. I enquired of them concerning the truth of this, and they said they knew nothing of it, further than that they had heard that it was the ancient custom among some nations. Their frequent changing of partners prevents propagation, creates disturbances, and often occasions murder and bloodshed; though this is commonly committed under pretense of being drunk. Their impunity to crimes committed when intoxicated with spirituous liquors, or their admitting one crime as an excuse for another, is a very unjust law or custom.

The extremes they run into in dividing the necessaries of life, are hurtful to the public weal; though their dividing meat when hunting, may answer a valuable purpose, as one family may have success one day, and the other the next; but their carrying this custom to the town, or to agriculture, is striking at the root of industry, as industrious persons ought to be rewarded, and the lazy suffer for their indolence.

They have scarcely any penal laws: the principal punishment is degrading: even murder is not punished by any formal law, only the friends of the murdered are at liberty to slay the murderer, if some atonement is not made. Their not annexing penalties to their laws, is perhaps not as great a crime, or as unjust and cruel, as the bloody penal laws of England, which we have so long shamefully practiced, and which are in force in this state, until our pentitentiary house is finished, which is now building, and then they are to be repealed.

Let us also take a view of the advantages attending Indian police:—They are not oppressed or perplexed with expensive litigation—They are not injured by legal robbery—They have no splendid villains that make themselves grand and great on other people's labor—They have neither church or state erected as money-making machines.

VI. HEAVEN AND EARTH

Man's need for a god to measure himself is as old as man himself.
From the European Christian viewpoint, were the Indians ir-
religious? How many gods did they worship? Of what sex were they?
Did the Indians believe in a life after death? in the immortality of the
soul? in heaven and hell? in the Creation? Was their religion a
substitute for science in explaining mysterious operations of Nature?
What was the role of their religious men? Were the Indians tolerant
of other beliefs? Were the Europeans tolerant of Indian beliefs?

James Smith, An Account of the Remarkable Occurrences in the
Life and Travels of Col. James Smith during his Captivity with the
Indians, in the years 1755, '56, '57, '58 & '59 *(Cincinnati, 1907).
pp. 143-148.*

As the family that I was adopted into was intermarried with the
Wiandots and Ottawas, three tongues were commonly spoke, viz.
Caughnewaga, or what the French call Iroque, also the Wiandot and
Ottawa; by this means I had an opportunity of learning these three
tongues; and I found that these nations varied in their traditions and
opinions concerning religion;—and even numbers of the same nations differed widely in their religious sentiments. Their traditions
are vague, whimsical, romantic and many of them scarce worth relating; and not any of them reach back to the creation of the world. The
Wiandots comes the nearest to this. They tell of a squaw that was
found when an infant, in the water in a canoe made of bull-rushes:
this squaw became a great prophetess and did many wonderful

things; she turned water into dry land, and at length made this continent, which was, at that time, only a very small island, and but a few
Indians in it. Tho they were then but few they had not sufficient
room to hunt; therefore this squaw went to the water side, and
prayed that this little island might be enlarged. The great being then
heard her prayer, and sent great numbers of Water Tortoises, and
Muskrats, which brought with them mud and other materials, for
enlarging this island, and by this means, they say, it was encreased to
the size that it now remains; therefore they say, that the white people
ought not to encroach upon them, or take their land from them, because their great grand mother made it.—They say, that about this
time the angels or heavenly inhabitants, as they call them, frequently
visited them and talked with their forefathers; and gave directions
how to pray, and how to appease the great being when he was offended. They told them that they were to offer sacrifice, burn tobacco, buffaloe and deer bones; but that they were not to burn bears or
racoons bones in sacrifice.

The Ottawas say, that there are two great beings that rule and
govern the universe, who are at war with each other; the one they call
Maneto, and the other *Matchemaneto*. They say that Maneto is all
kindness and love, and that Matchemaneto is an evil spirit, that
delights in doing mischief; and some of them think, that they are
equal in power, and therefore worship the evil spirit out of a principle
of fear. Others doubt which of the two may be the most powerful,
and therefore endeavor to keep in favor with both, by giving each of
them some kind of worship. Others say that Maneto is the first great
cause and therefore must be all-powerful and supreme, and ought to
be adored and worshipped; whereas Matchemaneto ought to be re-
jected and dispised.

Those of the Ottawas that worship the evil spirit, pretend to be
great conjurors. I think if there is any such thing now in the world as
witchcraft, it is among these people. I have been told wonderful
stories concerning their proceedings; but never was eye witness to
any thing that appeared evidently supernatural.

Some of the Wiandots and Caughnewagas profess to be Roman-
catholics; but even these retain many of the notions of their
ancestors. Those of them who reject the Roman-catholic religion,

hold that there is one great first cause, whom they call *Owaneeyo*, that rules and governs the universe, and takes care of all his creatures, rational and irrational, and gives them their food in due season, and hears the prayers of all those that call upon him; therefore it is but just and reasonable to pray, and offer sacrifice to this great being, and to do those things that are pleasing in his sight;—but they differ widely in what is pleasing or displeasing to this great being. Some hold that following nature or their own propensities is the way to happiness, and cannot be displeasing to the deity, because he delights in the happiness of his creatures, and does nothing in vain; but gave these dispositions with a design to lead to happiness, and therefore they ought to be followed. Others reject this opinion altogether, and say that following their own propensities in this manner, is neither the means of happiness nor the way to please the deity.

Tecaughretanego was of opinion that following nature in a limited sense was reasonable and right. He said that most of the irrational animals by following their natural propensities, were led to the greatest pitch of happiness that their natures and the world they lived in would admit of. He said that mankind and the rattle snakes had evil dispositions, that led them to injure themselves and others. He gave instances of this. He said he had a puppy that he did not intend to raise, and in order to try an experiment, he tyed this puppy on a pole and held it to a rattle snake, which bit it several times; that he observed the snake shortly after, rolling about apparently in great misery, so that it appeared to have poisoned itself as well as the puppy. The other instance he gave was concerning himself. He said that when he was a young man, he was very fond of the women, and at length got the venereal disease, so that by following this propensity, he was led to injure himself and others. He said our happiness depends on our using our reason, in order to suppress these evil dispositions; but when our propensities neither lead us to injure ourselves nor others, we might with safety indulge them, or even pursue them as the means of happiness.

The Indians generally are of opinion that there are great numbers of inferior Deities, which they call *Careyagaroona*, which signifies the Heavenly Inhabitants. These beings they suppose are employed as assistants, in managing the affairs of the universe, and in inspecting the actions of men: and that even the irrational animals are engaged in viewing their actions, and bearing intelligence to the Gods. The eagle, for this purpose, with her keen eye, is soaring about in the day, and the owl, with her nightly eye, perched on the trees around their camp in the night; therefore, when they observe the eagle or the owl near, they immediately offer sacrifice, or burn tobacco, that they may have a good report to carry to the Gods. They say that there are also great numbers of evil spirits, which they call *Onasahroona*, which signifies the Inhabitants of the Lower Region. These they say are employed in disturbing the world, and the good spirits are always going after them, and setting things right, so that they are constantly working in opposition to each other. Some talk of a future state, but not with any certainty: at best their notions are vague and unsettled. Others deny a future state altogether, and say that after death they neither think or live.

As the Caughnewagas and the six nations speak nearly the same language, their theology is also nearly alike. When I met with the Shawanees or Delawares, as I could not speak their tongue, I spoke Ottawa to them, and as it bore some resemblance to their language, we understood each other in some common affairs, but as I could only converse with them very imperfectly, I can not from my own knowledge, with certainty, give any account of their theological opinions.

Adriaen Van der Donck, A Description of the New Netherlands, *ed.* Thomas F. O'Donnell (Syracuse, 1968), pp. 102-109.

The natives are all heathen and without any religious devotions. Idols are neither known nor worshipped among them. When they take an oath they swear by the sun, which, they say, sees all things. They think much of the moon, and believe it has great influence over vegetation. Although they know all the planets from the other stars, by appropriate names, still they pay no idolatrous worship to the same, yet by the planets and other signs they are somewhat weatherwise. The offering up of prayers, or the making of any distinction

between days, or any matter of the kind, is unknown among them. They neither know or say any thing of God; but they possess great fear of the devil, who they believe causes diseases, and does them much injury. When they go on a hunting or fishing excursion they usually cast a part of what is first taken into the fire, without using any ceremony on the occasion, then saying, "stay thou devil, eat thou that." They love to hear us speak of God and of our religion, and are very attentive and still during divine service and prayers, and apparently are inclined to devotion; but in truth they know nothing about it, and live without any religion, or without any inward or outward godly fear, nor do they know of any superstition or idolatry; they only follow the instilled laws of nature, therefore some suppose they can easily be brought to the knowledge and fear of God. Among some nations the word Sunday is known by the name of *Kintowen*. The oldest among them say that in former times the knowledge and fear of God had been known among them, and they remark, that since they can neither read nor write, in process of time the Sunday will be forgotten, and all knowledge of the same lost. Their old men, when we reason earnestly with them on the matter, seem to feel pensive or sorrowful, but manifest no other emotions or agitations—when we reprove them for bad conduct and reason with them on its impropriety, and say that there is a God in heaven above whom they offend, their common answer is, "We do not know that God, we have never seen him, we know not who he is—if you know him and fear him, as you say you do, how does it then happen that so many thieves, drunkards, and evil-doers are found among you. Certainly that G   ill punish you severely, because he has warned you to bew   e deeds, which he has never done to us. We know
r   nd therefore we do not deserve such punishment."
                       adopt our religion, nor have there been any
                       for their conversion. When their children
                    re frequently taken into our families for
                   g to opportunity, instructed in our
                   rown up, and turn lovers and asso-
                   forget their religious impressions
                   suits have taken great pains
                   ans to the Roman Church,

and outwardly many profess that religion; but inasmuch as they are not well instructed in its fundamental principles, they fall off lightly and make sport of the subject and its doctrine.

In the year 1639, when a certain merchant, who is still living with us, went into that country to trade with an Indian chief who spoke good French, after he had drank two or three glasses of wine, they began to converse on the subject of religion. The chief said that he had been instructed so far that he often said mass among the Indians, and that on a certain occasion the place where the altar stood caught fire by accident, and our people made preparations to put out the fire, which he forbade them to do, saying that God, who stands there, is almighty, and he will put out the fire himself and we waited with great attention, but the fire continued till all was burned up, with your almighty God himself and with all the fine things about him. Since that time I have never held to that religion, but regard the sun and moon much more, as being better than all your Gods are; for they warm the earth and cause the fruits to grow, when your lovely Gods cannot preserve themselves from the fire. In the whole country I know no more than one Indian who is firm in his religious profession, nor can any change be expected among them, as long as matters are permitted to remain as heretofore. If they are to be brought over to the Christian faith, then the public hand must be extended to them and continued; we must establish good schools at convenient places among them, for the instruction of their children; let them learn to write our catechism, and let them be thoroughly instructed in the fundamental principles of our religion, so that in process of time they may be enabled to instruct each other and become attached thereto. It certainly would be attended with some trouble and expense to the government, still, without such means and measures, it will be difficult to do any good among them. Our negligence on those matters is very reprehensible, for the Indians themselves say that they are very desirous to have their children instructed in our language and religion.

OF THEIR HOPE AFTER THIS PRESENT LIFE

It is a wonderful truth which affords strong evidence
believers and free-thinking spirits that this barb

people of whom we have treated should know that there is a distinction between the body and the soul, and believe, as they actually do, that the one is perishable and the other immortal. The soul, they say, is that spirit which directs all the actions of the body, and is the producing cause of all good and evil conduct, which, when the body dies, separates from it and removes to a place towards the south, where the climate is so fine that no covering against the cold will be necessary, and where the heat will never be troublesome. To this place the souls of all those who have been good and valuable in this life will go, where they will be satisfied and have an abundance of good things, without any trouble or labour for the same, forever; and they who have been bad in this life after death will go to another place, where their condition will be directly contrary to the first; where they will never enjoy peace and contentment, as the good will do. But I have never been able rightly to discover whether they believe the soul will be hereafter united to the body. I have, however, spoken with Christians who remark that they have heard them state such to be their belief. But they do not affirm to this fact. When they hear voices or noises in the woods at night, which frequently happens, and which, we believe, usually proceed from wild animals, but which they declare, with fear and astonishment, are made by the wicked, the souls of whom are thus doomed to wander at night in the woods and solitary places for punishment in unhappy situations. The Indians, because they fear those subjects, do not travel by night unless it be necessary, and then go in parties or companies; when they go alone they always carry a fire-brand with them, with which they believe they can keep off those evil spirits and prevent them from doing them any injury, which, they say, are always disposed to frighten them and do them wrong. They acknowledge also that the soul proceeds from God, and that the same is his gift. This we sometimes learn from their old men of understanding, when an opportunity presents itself in conversation, and we probably would discover more of them in relation to this matter if we did perfectly understand their languages. Among their common or young people we do not hear those spoken of. In this we still see the providence of God, who, by the common light of nature, has given to this people the knowledge that there is, after this life, a reward for the just, and a punishment for the unjust, which all mankind may expect.

OF THEIR KNOWLEDGE OF GOD AND
THEIR FEAR OF THE DEVILS

Although the original inhabitants of the New Netherlands be heathen and are unbelievers, they however believe and acknowledge that there is a God in heaven from all eternity, who is almighty. But they say God is good, kind, and compassionate, who will not punish or do any injury to any person, and therefore takes no concern himself in the common affairs of the world, nor does he meddle with the same, except that he has ordered the devil to take care of those matters. For they say that all which happens to persons on the earth is ordered and directed by the devil as he pleases. God, the chief of all, who dwells in heaven, is much greater and higher than the devil, over whom he has power, but he will not meddle in, or trouble himself with, those concerns.

When, on those subjects, we answer them conclusively that the devil is deceitful and wicked, they acknowledge it to be true, and that he to the extent of his powers directs such matters in the most wicked and injurious ways (wherein he takes pleasure). They say that all accidents, infirmities, and diseases, are sent and forced upon them by the devil, to whom they ascribe it by the common name, saying that the devil is in them, and is the cause of all their misfortunes and ailments. For instance, if they have any inward complaint, they say there is a devil in me; if they have a defect in arm or leg, foot, or hand, shoulder or in the head, they devote the part, and say there is a devil in the same. And because he is so unkind to them, they must, whether they be willing or not, fear him, and preserve his friendship, and sometimes (as before related) cast a piece to him into the fire. Where we refute those follies, by saying that God knows all things, and is almighty, and has a perfect knowledge of the devil, and observes his conduct, and will not permit him to rule over man, who is created in the image of God, and is the noblest part of the creation; nor will the devil be permitted to tyrannize over man, provided they will rightly confide and trust in God, and not withdraw from his commandments to do evil; then they repay us, with strange and fabulous replies, saying, "You lazy Dutchmen say so, and when we observe the matter outwardly it would appear to be true—what you say; but in fact you do not understand the matter. That God, who is the highest good, almighty and gracious, and Lord of heaven and earth, in whom all power is, exists in heaven, but not alone, and without pasttime; for he has there with him a goddess, a female person, the most beautiful ever known and beheld. With this goddess or beautiful person he is so much engrossed that the time is passed away and forgotten. Meantime the devil plays the tyrant and does what he pleases.''

This belief and feeling is deeply impressed in them, and when we with stronger reasons sift the subject and drive them from their positions, they fall into more abominable absurdities, and like the dogs return to their vomit, and say they must serve the devil because he has the power to do them injuries.

THEIR OPINIONS OF THE CREATION, &c.

From the young Indians who frequent our settlements, and continue somewhat wild, we cannot derive any certain information of their belief on these matters; but we must have recourse to their aged men of understanding when we desire to know their belief on these important subjects.

It sometimes happens when we enter into a curious discourse with them that they ask us our opinions on the origin of man, and how they came to this country; and when we inform them in broken language of the creation of Adam, they cannot believe, or will not understand relative to their people and the negroes, on account of their great difference and the inequality of colour. According to their opinion the world was not created as described in the first and second chapters of the book of Genesis; but they say the world was before all mountains, men, and animals; that God then was with that beautiful woman, who now is with him, without knowing when or from whence they came; then was all water, or the water covered all; and they add that if there had been any eyes in being, there was nothing but water to be seen, and nothing else visible in every direction.

It happened at this period, they say, that the before mentioned beautiful woman or goddess gradually descended from heaven, even into the water, gross or corpulent like a woman who apparently would bring forth more than one child. Having gradually settled into the water, she did not go under it; but immediately at the place where she descended some land appeared under her, whereon she remained sitting. This land increased, and in time became greater and dry around the place where she sat; like one who is placed on a bar, whereon the water is three or four feet deep, which by the ebbing of the tide becomes dry land.

Thus they say and mean to be understood, it occurred with this descended goddess. And that the land became of greater extent around her, until its extent was unbounded to the sight, when vegetation appeared; and in time fruitful and unfruitful trees began to grow throughout the world as it now appears. Whether the world of which you speak originated at this time, we cannot say.

At this period of time, when those things had taken place and were accomplished, this great person was overtaken in labour and brought forth three distinct and different creatures. The first was like a deer as those now are, the second like a bear, and the third like a wolf in every respect. The woman suckled those animals to maturity, and remained a considerable time upon the earth, cohabiting with those several animals, and bringing forth at every birth more than one of a different species and appearance; from which have originated and proceeded all the human beings, animals and creatures, of every description and species, as the same now are and appear; being propagated according to nature, each in their peculiar order, as the same are in succession continued.

When all those subjects were brought to a state of perfection, and could continue, this common mother rejoiced greatly and ascended up to heaven, where she will continue to remain and dwell, enjoying pleasure, and subsist in goodness and love, which her upper Lord will afford her, for which she is particularly desirous, and God also loves her supremely above all things.

Here on the earth, in the meanwhile, the human species, and the animals after their kind, have multiplied and produced so many different creatures, and increased exceedingly, which every other thing that was created also does, as the same at present is seen. Therefore it is at this time that all mankind, wherever they be, are always born with the nature of one or the other of the aforesaid animals. They are timid and innocent like the deer; they are brave, revengeful, and just of hand, like the bear; or they are deceitful and bloodthirsty, like the wolves. Although their dispositions are apparently somewhat changed, this they attribute to the subtlety of men, who know how to conceal their wicked propensities.

This, they say, is all they have learned from their fathers on the subject of the Creation, which has been handed down to them, and which they believe to be true. And they add if they had been able to write as you are, they would have transmitted and left us all the particulars on these matters, which they could not do, because they know not the art of writing.

Robert Beverley, The History and Present State of Virginia, *ed. David Freeman Hawke (Indianapolis, 1971), pp. 102-111.*

I have been at several of the Indian towns and conversed with some of the most sensible of them in that country, but I could learn little from them, it being reckoned sacrilege to divulge the principles of their religion. However, the following adventure discovered something of it: As I was ranging the woods with some other friends, we fell upon their quioccasan (which is their house of religious worship) at a time when the whole town were gathered together in another place to consult about the bounds of the land given them by the English.

Thus finding ourselves masters of so fair an opportunity (because we knew the Indians were engaged) we resolved to make use of it and to examine their quioccasan, the inside of which they never suffer any Englishman to see. And having removed about fourteen logs from the door with which it was barricadoed, we went in and at first found nothing but naked walls and a fireplace in the middle. This house was about eighteen foot wide and thirty foot long, built after the manner of their other cabins but larger, with a hole in the middle of the roof to vent the smoke, the door being at one end. Round about the house at some distance from it were set up posts with faces carved on them and painted. We did not observe any window or passage for the light except the door and the vent of the chimney. At last we observed that at the farther end about ten foot of the room was cut off by a partition of very close mats, and it was dismal dark behind that partition. We were at first scrupulous to enter this obscure place, but at last we ventured, and groping about we felt some posts in the middle. Then reaching our hands up those posts we found large shelves, and upon these shelves three mats, each of which was rolled up and sewed fast. These we handed down to the light, and to save time in unlacing the seams we made use of a knife and ripped them without doing any damage to the mats. In one of these we found some vast bones which we judged to be the bones of men. Particularly we measured one thighbone and found it two foot nine inches long. In another mat we found some Indian tomahawks finely graved and painted. Among these tomahawks was the largest that ever I saw. There was fastened to it a wild turkey's beard painted red, and two of the longest feathers of his wings hung dangling at it by a string of about six inches long tied to the end of the tomahawk. In the third mat there was something which we took to be their idol, tho' of an underling sort and wanted putting together. The pieces were these: First, a board three foot and a half long with one indenture at the upper end like a fork to fasten the head upon; from thence half way down were half hoops nailed to the edges of the board at about four inches distance, which were bowed out to represent the breast and belly; on the lower half was another board of half the length of the other, fastened to it by joints or pieces of wood which being set on each side stood out about fourteen inches from the body and half as high. We supposed the use of these to be for the bowing out of the knees when the image was set up. There were packed up with these things red and blue pieces of cotton cloth and rolls made up for arms, thighs, and legs bent to at the knees. It would be difficult to see one of these images at this day because the Indians are extreme shy of exposing them. We put the cloths upon the hoops for the body and fastened on the arms and legs to have a view of the representation, but the head and rich bracelets which it is usually adorned with were not there or at least we did not find them. We had not leisure to make a very narrow search, for having spent about an hour in this inquiry we feared the business of the Indians might be near over, and that if we stayed longer we might be caught offering an affront to their superstition. For this reason we wrapped up these holy materials in their several mats again and laid them on the shelf where we found them. This image when dressed up might look very venerable in that dark place where 'tis not possible to see it but by the glimmering light that is let in by lifting up a piece of the matting, which we observed to be conveniently hung for that purpose. For when the light of the door and chimney glance in several directions upon the image thro' that little passage, it must needs make a strange representation which those poor people are taught to worship with a devout ignorance. There are other things that contribute towards carrying on this imposture: First, the chief conjurer enters within the partition in the dark and may undiscerned move the image as he pleases; secondly, a priest of authority stands in the room with the people to keep them from being too inquisitive, under the penalty of the deity's displeasure and his own censure.

Their idol bears a several name in every nation—as Okee, Quioccos, Kiwasa. They do not look upon it as one single being but reckon there are many of them of the same nature. They likewise believe that there are tutelar deities in every town.

Once in my travels in very cold weather I met at an Englishman's house with an Indian of whom an extraordinary character had been given me for his ingenuity and understanding. When I see he had no other Indian with him, I thought I might be the more free, and therefore I made much of him—seating him close by a large fire, and giving him plenty of strong cider which I hoped would make him good company and openhearted. After I found him well warmed (for unless they be surprised some way or other they will not talk freely of their religion) I asked him concerning their God and what their notions of him were? He freely told me they believed God was universally beneficent, that his dwelling was in the heavens above, and that the influences of his goodness reached to the earth beneath; that he was incomprehensible in his excellence and enjoyed all possible felicity, that his duration was eternal, his perfection boundless, and that he possesses everlasting indolence and ease. I told him I had heard that they worshiped the devil and asked why they did not rather worship God whom they had so high an opinion of and who would give them all good things and protect them from any mischief that the devil could do them? To this his answer was that 'tis true God is the giver of all good things, but they flow naturally and promiscuously from him; that they are showered down upon all men indifferently without distinction; that God does not trouble himself with the impertinent affairs of men, nor is concerned at what they do, but leaves them to make the most of their free will and to secure as many as they can of the good things that flow from him. That therefore it was to no purpose either to fear or worship him; but on the contrary if they did not pacify the evil spirit and make him propitious, he would take away or spoil all those good things that God had given and ruin their health, their peace, and their plenty by sending war, plague, and famine among them. For, said he, this evil spirit is always busying himself with our affairs and frequently visiting us, being present in the air, in the thunder, and in the storms. He told me farther that he expected adoration and sacrifice from them on pain of his displeasure, and that therefore they thought it convenient to make their court to him. I then asked him concerning the image which they worship in their quioccasan and assured him that it was a dead, insensible log equipped with a bundle of clouts, a mere helpless thing made by men that could neither hear, see, nor speak; and that such a stupid thing could no ways hurt or help them. To this he answered very unwillingly and with much hesitation. However, he at last delivered himself in these broken and imperfect sentences: "It is the priests—they make the people believe and—" Here he paused a little and then repeated to me that "it was the priests—" and then gave me hopes that he would have said something more, but a qualm crossed his conscience and hindered him from making any further concession.

The priests and conjurers have a great sway in every nation. Their words are looked upon as oracles and consequently are of great weight among the common people. They perform their adorations and conjurations in the general language before spoken of, as the Catholics of all nations do their mass in the Latin. They teach that the souls of men survive their bodies, and that those who have done well here enjoy most transporting pleasures in their Elysium hereafter; that this Elysium is stored with the highest perfection of all their earthly pleasures—namely, with plenty of all sorts of game for hunting, fishing, and fowling; that it is blest with the most charming women which enjoy an eternal bloom and have a universal desire to please; that it is delivered from excesses of cold or heat and flourishes with an everlasting spring. But that on the contrary those who are wicked and live scandalously here are condemned to a filthy, stinking lake after death that continually burns with flames that never extinguish, where they are persecuted and tormented day and night with furies in the shape of old women.

They use many divinations and enchantments and frequently offer burnt sacrifice to the evil spirit. The people annually present their first fruits of every season and kind; namely, of birds, beasts, fish, fruits, plants, roots, and of all other things which they esteem either of profit or pleasure to themselves. They repeat their offerings as frequently as they have great successes in their wars or their fishing, fowling, or hunting.

Some few years ago there happened a very dry time towards the heads of the rivers and especially on the upper parts of James River where Colonel Byrd had several quarters of Negroes. This gentleman has for a long time been extremely respected and feared by all the Indians round about, who, without knowing the name of any governor, have ever been kept in order by him. During this drought an Indian well known to one of the colonel's overseers came to him and asked if his tobacco was not like to be spoiled? The overseer answered yes, if they had not rain very suddenly. The Indian, who pretended great kindness for his master, told the overseer if he would promise to give him two bottles of rum he would bring him rain enough. The overseer did not believe anything of the matter, not seeing at that time the least appearance of rain nor so much as a cloud in the sky. However, he promised to give him the rum when his master came thither if he would be as good as his word. Upon this the Indian went immediately a-pow-wowing, as they call it, and in about half an hour there came up a black cloud into the sky that showered down rain enough upon this gentleman's corn and tobacco, but none at all upon any of the neighbors except a few drops of the skirt of the shower. The Indian for that time went away without returning to the overseer again till he heard of his master's arrival at the falls, and then he came to him and demanded the two bottles of rum. The colonel at first seemed to know nothing of the matter and asked the Indian for what reason he made that demand (altho' his overseer had been so overjoyed at what had happened that he could not rest till he had taken a horse and rid near forty miles to tell his master the story). The Indian answered with some concern that he hoped the overseer had let him know the service he had done him by bringing a shower of rain to save his crop. At this the colonel, not being apt to believe such stories, smiled and told him he was a cheat and had seen the cloud a-coming, otherwise he could neither have brought rain nor so much as foretold it. The Indian, at this seeming much troubled, replied: "Why, then, had not such a one and such a one (naming the next neighbors) rain as well as your overseer, for they lost their crops; but I loved you and therefore saved yours?" The colonel made sport with him a little while, but in the end ordered him the two bottles of rum, letting him understand, however, that it was a free gift and not the consequence of any bargain with his overseer.

The solemnity of huskanawing is commonly practiced once every fourteen or sixteen years or oftener as their young men happen to grow up. It is an institution or discipline which all young men must pass before they can be admitted to be of the number of the great men or cockarouses of the nation. The whole ceremony is performed after the following manner.

The choicest and briskest young men of the town and such only as have acquired some treasure by their travels and hunting are chosen out by the rulers to be huskanawed, and whoever refuses to undergo this process dare not remain among them. The principal part of the business is to carry them into the woods and there keep them under confinement and destitute of all society for several months, giving them no other sustenance but the infusion or decoction of some poisonous intoxicating roots; by virtue of which physic and by the severity of the discipline which they undergo they become stark staring mad, in which raving condition they are kept eighteen or twenty days. During these extremities they are shut up night and day in a strong enclosure made on purpose; one of which I saw, belonging to the Paumunkey Indians, in the year 1694. It was in shape like a sugar loaf and every way open like a lattice for the air to pass through. In this cage thirteen young men had been huskanawed and had not been a month set at liberty when I saw it. Upon this occasion it is pretended that these poor creatures drink so much of that water of Lethe that they perfectly lose the remembrance of all former things, even of their parents, their treasure, and their language. When the doctors find that they have drank sufficiently of the wysoccan (so they call this made potion) they gradually restore them to their senses again by lessening the intoxication of their diet. But before they are perfectly well they bring them back into their towns while they are still wild and crazy through the violence of the medicine. After this they are very fearful of discovering anything of their former remembrance, for if such a thing should happen to any of them, they must immediately be huskanawed again, and the second time the usage is so severe that seldom anyone escapes with life. Thus they must pretend to have forgot the very use of their tongues so as not to be able to speak nor understand anything that is spoken till they learn it again. Now whether this be real or counterfeit I don't know, but certain it is that they will not for some time take notice of anybody nor anything with which they were before acquainted, being still under the guard of their keepers, who constantly wait upon them everywhere till they have learnt all things perfectly over again. Thus they unlive their former lives and commence men by forgetting that they ever have been boys.

I can account no other way for the great pains and secrecy of the keepers during the whole process of this discipline but by assuring you that it is the most meritorious thing in the world to discharge that trust well in order to their preferment to the greatest posts in the nation, which they claim as their undoubted right in the next promotion. On the other hand, they are sure of a speedy passport into the other world if they should by their levity or neglect show themselves in the least unfaithful.

Those which I ever observed to have been huskanawed were lively, handsome, well timbered young men from fifteen to twenty years of age or upward, and such as were generally reputed rich.

I confess I judged it at first sight to be only an invention of the seniors to engross the young men's riches to themselves, for after suffering this operation they never pretended to call to mind anything of their former property. But their goods were either shared among the old men or brought to some public use, and so those younkers [young gentlemen] were obliged to begin the world again.

But the Indians detest this opinion and pretend that this violent method of taking away the memory is to release the youth from all their childish impressions and from that strong partiality to persons and things which is contracted before reason comes to take place.

They hope by this proceeding to root out all the prepossessions and unreasonable prejudices which are fixed in the minds of children, so that when the young men come to themselves again their reason may act freely without being bypassed by the cheats of custom and education. Thus also they become discharged from the remembrance of any ties by blood and are established in a state of equality and perfect freedom to order their actions and dispose of their persons as they think fit without any other control than that of the law of nature. By this means also they become qualified when they have any public office equally and impartially to administer justice without having friend or relation.

The Indians offer sacrifice almost upon every new occasion—as when they travel or begin a long journey, they burn tobacco instead of incense to the sun to bribe him to send them fair weather and a prosperous voyage. When they cross any great water or violent fresh or torrent they throw tobacco, puccoon, peak, or some other valuable thing that they happen to have about them to entreat the spirit presiding there to grant them a safe passage. It is called a fresh when after very great rains or (as we suppose) after a great thaw of the snow and ice lying upon the mountains to the northwest the water descends in such abundance into the rivers that they overflow the banks which bound their streams at other times.

They make their account by units—tens, hundreds, etc.—as we do, but they reckon the years by the winters, or cohonks as they call them, which is a name taken from the note of the wild geese, intimating so many times of the wild geese coming to them, which is every winter. They distinguish the several parts of the year by five seasons, viz., the budding or blossoming of the spring; the earing of the corn or roasting ear time; the summer or highest sun; the corn gathering or fall of the leaf; and the winter or cohonks. They count the months likewise by the moons, tho' not with any relation to so many in a year as we do, but they make them return again by the same name, as the Moon of Stags, the Corn Moon, the first and second moon of cohonks, etc. They have no distinction of the hours of the day, but divide it only into three parts—the rise, power, and lowering of the sun. And they keep their account by knots on a string or notches on a stick, not unlike the Peruvian quippoes.

In this state of nature one would think they should be as pure from superstition and overdoing matters in religion as they are in other things; but I find it is quite the contrary, for this simplicity gives the cunning priest a greater advantage over them, according to the Romish maxim, "Ignorance is the mother of devotion." For no bigoted pilgrim appears more zealous or strains his devotion more at the shrine than these believing Indians do in their idolatrous adorations. Neither do the most refined Catholics undergo their penance with so much submission as these poor pagans do the severities which their priests inflict upon them.

The conjurer is a partner with the priest not only in the cheat but in the advantages of it, and sometimes they officiate for one another. When this artist is in the act of conjuration, or of pow-wowing as they term it, he always appears with an air of haste or else in some convulsive posture that seems to strain all the faculties, like the sybils when they pretend to be under the power of inspiration. At these times he has a black bird with expanded wings fastened to his ear, differing in nothing but color from Mahomet's pigeon. He has no clothing but a small skin before and a pocket at his girdle.

The Indians never go about any considerable enterprise without first consulting their priests and conjurers, for the most ingenious amongst them are brought up to those functions, and by that means become better instructed in their histories than the rest of the people. They likewise engross to themselves all the knowledge of nature which is handed to them by tradition from their forefathers, by which means they are able to make a truer judgment of things and consequently are more capable of advising those that consult them upon all occasions. These reverend gentlemen are not so entirely given up to their religious austerities but they sometimes take their pleasure (as well as the laity) in fishing, fowling, and hunting.

The Indians have posts fixed round their quioccasan which have men's faces carved upon them and are painted. They are likewise set up round some of their other celebrated places and make a circle for them to dance about on certain solemn occasions. They very often set up pyramidical stones and pillars which they color with puccoon and other sorts of paint, and which they adorn with peak, roanoke, etc. To these they pay all outward signs of worship and devotion, not as to God, but as they are hieroglyphics of the permanency and immutability of the deity—because these both for figure and substance are of all sublunary bodies the least subject to decay or change. They also for the same reason keep baskets of stones in their cabins. Upon this account, too, they offer sacrifice to running streams, which by the perpetuity of their motion typify the eternity of God.

VII. DEATH

To everything, said the Preacher, there is a season, a time to be born and a time to die. Did the Indians fear death? Did they believe in euthanasia (mercy killing)? What were Indian funerals like? What was their social function? How were Indians buried? Why? Were all persons given the same kind of funeral? Were the dead mourned? Were there any expenses for a funeral? Who paid? How did the Christian observers regard Indian customs of death?

John Long, Voyages and Travels of an Indian Interpreter and Trader, *ed. Milo Milton Quaife (Chicago, 1922), pp. 95-97.*

Death among the Indians, in many situations, is rather courted than dreaded, and particularly at an advanced period of life, when they have not strength or activity to hunt. The father then solicits to change his climate, and the son cheerfully acts the part of an executioner, putting a period to his parent's existence.

Among the northern Chippewas, when the father of a family seems reluctant to comply with the usual custom and his life becomes burdensome to himself and friends, and his children are obliged to maintain him with the labor of their hands, they propose to him the alternative, either to be put on shore on some island, with a small canoe and paddles, bows and arrows, and a bowl to drink out of, and there run the risk of starving, or to suffer death according to the laws of the nation, manfully. As there are few instances where the latter is not preferred, I shall relate the ceremony practiced on such an occasion.

A sweating-house is prepared in the same form as at the ceremony of adoption, and whilst the person is under this preparatory trial, the family are rejoicing that the Master of Life has communicated to them the knowledge of disposing of the aged and infirm, and sending them to a better country, where they will be renovated and hunt again with all the vigor of youth. They then smoke the pipe of peace, and have their dog feast. They also sing the grand medicine song, as follows:

"*Wa haguarmissey Kitchee Mannitoo kaygait cockinor nishinnor-bay ojey kee candan hepadgey kee zargetoone nishinnorbay mor-nooch kee tarpenan nocey keen aighter, O, dependan nishinnorbay, mornooch towwarch weene ojey mishcoot pockcan tunnockay.*" "The Master of Life gives courage. It is true, all Indians know that he loves us, and we now give our father to him, that he may find himself young in another country and be able to hunt."

The songs and dances are renewed, and the eldest son gives his father the death stroke with a tomahawk. They then take the body, which they paint in the best manner and bury it with the war weapons, making a bark hut to cover the grave, to prevent the wild animals from disturbing it.

Thus do the unenlightened part of mankind assume a privilege of depriving each other of life, when it can no longer be supported by the labor of their own hands, and think it a duty to put a period to the existence of those to whom they are indebted for their own, and employ those arms to give the fatal stroke, which in more civilized countries would have been exerted for their support.

Adriaen Van der Donck, A Description of the New Netherlands, *ed. Thomas F. O'Donnell (Syracuse, 1968), pp. 86-88.*

Whenever an Indian departs this life, all the residents of the place assemble at the funeral. To a distant stranger, who has not a friend or relative in the place, they pay the like respect. They are equally careful to commit the body to the earth, without neglecting any of the usual ceremonies, according to the standing of the deceased. In deadly diseases, they are faithful to sustain and take care of each other. Whenever a soul has departed, the nearest relatives extend the limbs and close the eyes of the dead; and after the body has been watched and wept over several days and nights, they bring it to the grave, wherein they do not lay it down, but place it in a sitting posture upon a stone or a block of wood, as if the body were sitting upon a stool; then they place a pot, kettle, platter, spoon, with some provision and money, near the body in the grave; this they say is necessary for the journey to the other world. Then they place as much wood around the body as will keep the earth from it. Above the grave they place a large pile of wood, stone or earth, and around and above the same they place palisades resembling a small dwelling. All their burial places are secluded and preserved with religious veneration and care, and they consider it wicked and infamous to disturb or injure their burial places. The nearest relatives of the deceased, particularly the women (the men seldom exhibit much excitement), have their periods of lamentations, when they make dreadful and wonderful wailing, naming the dead, smiting upon their breasts, scratching and disfiguring their faces, and showing all possible signs of grief. But where a mother has lost a child, her expressions of grief exceed all bounds, for she calls and wails whole nights over her infant, as if she really were in a state of madness. If the deceased are young persons, or persons slain in war, then their lamentations are of a particular kind, and the women shave off their hair, which they keep the customary time, and then they burn the hair upon the graves of the deceased or slain, in the presence of the relations. In short they possess strong passions and exhibit the same with much feeling when mourning over their dead relatives and friends. For the purpose of removing the existing causes of grief, and not to excite sorrow in the mind of the bereaved; and as far as possible to promote forgetfulness of the friends lost, the name of the deceased is never mentioned in the presence of the relations; or when the name is mentioned, it is received as if designed to produce mortification, and as an act of unkindness. The use of tokens of mourning is common, which usually are black signs upon their bodies; when a woman loses her husband, she shaves off her hair, and paints her whole countenance black as pitch, and men do the same when their wives die, and they also wear a buckskin vest next to their skin, and mourn a whole year, even if they have not been long married, or if the connection had not been happy—still they observe the ceremonies religiously, without marrying again until the season of mourning is over.

John Lawson, A New Voyage to Carolina (*Richmond, 1937*), *pp. 190-193*.

The Burial of their Dead is performed with a great deal of Ceremony, in which one Nation differs in some few Circumstances from another, yet not so much but we may, by a general Relation, pretty nearly account for them all.

When an Indian is dead the greater Person he was, the more expensive is his Funeral. The first thing which is done, is to place the nearest Relations near the Corps, who mourn and weep very much, having their Hair hanging down their Shoulders in a very forlorn manner. After the dead Person has lain a Day and a Night in one of their Hurdles of Canes, commonly in some Out-House made for that purpose, those that officiate about the Funeral go into the Town, and the first young Men they meet withal, that have Blankets or Match Coats on, whom they think fit for their Turn, they strip them from their Backs, who suffer them so to do without any Resistance. In these they wrap the dead Bodies, and cover them with two or three Mats which the Indians make of Rushes or Cane; and last of all, they have a long Web of woven Reeds or hollow Canes, which is the coffin of the Indians, and is brought round several times and tied fast at both ends, which, indeed, looks very decent and well. Then the Corps is brought out of the House into the Orchard of Peach-Trees, where another Hurdle is made to receive it, about which comes all the Relations and Nation that the dead Person belonged to, besides several from other Nations in Alliance with them; all which sit down on the Ground upon Mats spread there for that purpose; where the Doctor or Conjurer appears; and, after some time, makes a Sort of O-yes, at which all are very silent, then he begins to give an Account who the dead Person was, and how stout a Man he approved himself; how many Enemies and Captives he had killed and taken; how strong, tall, and nimble he was; that he was a great Hunter; a Lover of his Country, and possessed of a great many beautiful Wives and Children, esteemed the greatest of Blessings among these Savages, in which they have a true Notion. Thus this Orator runs on, highly extoling the Dead Man for his Valor, Conduct, Strength, Riches, and

Good-Humour; and enumerating his Guns, Slaves, and almost everything he was possessed of when living. After which he addresses himself to the People of that Town or Nation, and bids them supply the
dead Man's Place by following his steps, who, he assures them, is
gone into the Country of Souls, (which they think lies a great way off
in this World which the Sun visits in his ordinary Course,) and that
he will have the Enjoyment of handsome young Women, great Store
of Deer to hunt, never meet with Hunger, Cold or Fatigue, but everything to answer his Expectation and Desire. This is the Heaven they
propose to themselves; but, on the contrary, for those Indians that
are lazy, thievish amongst themselves, bad Hunters, and no War-
riours, nor of much Use to the Nation, to such they allot, in the next
World, Hunger, Cold, Troubles, old ugly Women for their Companions, with Snakes, and all sorts of nasty Victuals to feed on. Thus is
marked out their Heaven and Hell. After all this Harangue, he
diverts the People with some of their Traditions, as when there was a
violent hot Summer, or very hard Winter; when any notable Distempers raged amongst them; when they were at War with such and such
Nations; how victorious they were; and what were the Names of their
War-Captains. To prove the times more exactly, he produces the
Records of the Country, which are a Parcel of Reeds of different
Lengths, with several distinct Marks, known to none but themselves,
by which they seem to guess very exactly at Accidents that happened
many Years ago; nay, two or three Ages or more. The Reason I have
to believe what they tell me on this Account, is, because I have been
at the Meetings of several Indian Nations, and they agreed, in relating the same Circumstances as to Time, very exactly; as for Example, they say there was so hard a Winter in Carolina 105 Years ago,
that the great Sound was frozen over, and the Wild Geese came into
the Woods to eat Acorns, and that they were so tame, (I suppose
through Want) that they killed abundance in the Woods by knocking
them on the Head with Sticks.

But to return to the dead Man. When this long Tale is ended, by
him that spoke first; perhaps a second begins another long Story; so a
third, and fourth, if there be so many Doctors present; which all tell
one and the same thing. At last the Corps is brought away from that
Hurdle to the Grave by four young Men, attended by the Relations,
the King, old Men, and all the Nation. When they come to the Sepul-

chre, which is about six Foot deep and eight Foot long, having at each end (that is, at the Head and Foot) a Light-Wood or Pitch-Pine Fork driven close down the sides of the Grave firmly into the Ground; (these two Forks are to contain a Ridge-Pole, as you shall understand presently) before they lay the Corps into the Grave, they cover the bottom two or three times over with Bark of Trees, then they let down the Corps (with two Belts, that the Indians carry their Burdens withal) very Leisurely upon the said Barks; then they lay over a Pole of the same Wood in the two Forks, and having a great many Pieces of Pitch-Pine Logs, about two Foot and a half long, they stick them in the sides of the Grave down each End and near the Top thereof, where the other Ends lie on the Ridge-Pole, so that they are declining like the Roof of a House. These being very thick placed, they cover them (many times double) with Bark; then they throw the Earth thereon that came out of the Grave, and beat it down very firm; by this Means the dead Body lies in a Vault, nothing touching him; so that when I saw this way of Burial I was mightily pleased with it, esteeming it very decent and pretty, as having seen a great many Christians buried without the tenth Part of that Ceremony and Decency. Now, when the Flesh is rotted and moulded from the Bone, they take up the Carcass and clean the Bones and joint them together; afterwards they dress them up in pure white dressed Deer-Skins, and lay them amongst their Grandees and Kings in the Quiogonzon, which is their Royal Tomb or Burial-Place of their Kings and War-Captains. This is a very large magnificent Cabin, (according to their Building) which is raised at the Public Charge of the Nation, and maintained in a great deal of Form and Neatness. About seven Foot high is a Floor or Loft made, on which lie all their Princes and Great Men that have died for several hundred Years, all attired in the Dress I before told you of. No Person is to have his Bones lie here, and to be thus dressed, unless he gives a round Sum of their Money to the Rulers for Admittance. If they remove never so far, to live in a Foreign Country, they never fail to take all these dead Bones along with them, though the Tediousness of their short daily Marches keeps them never so long on their Journey. They reverence and adore this Quiogozon with all the Veneration and Respect that is possible for such a People to discharge, and had rather lose all than have any Violence or Injury offered thereto.

These Savages differ some small matter in their Burials; some burying right upwards, and otherwise, as you are acquainted withal in my Journal from South to North Carolina; Yet they all agree in the Mourning, which is, to appear every Night at the Sepulchre, and howl and weep in a very dismal manner, having their Faces dawbed over with Light-Wood Soot, (which is the same as Lampblack) and Bear's Oil. This renders them as black as it is possible to make themselves, so that theirs very much resemble the Faces of Executed Men boiled in Tar. If the dead Person was a Grandee, to carry on the Funeral Ceremonies, they hire People to cry and lament over the dead Man. Of this sort there are several that practice it for a Livelihood, and are very expert at Shedding abundance of Tears, and howling like Wolves, and so discharging their Office with abundance of Hypocrisy and Art. The Women are never accompanied with these Ceremonies after Death, and to what World they allot that Sex, I never understood, unless to wait on their dead Husbands: but they have more Wit than some of the other Eastern Nations, who sacrifice themselves to accompany their Husbands into the next World. It is the dead Man's Relations by Blood as his Uncles, Brothers, Sisters, Cousins, Sons and Daughters, that mourn in good earnest, the Wives thinking their Duty is discharged, and that they are become free, when their Husband is dead; so as fast as they can look out for another to supply his Place.

John Heckewelder, An Account of the History, Manners, and Customs, of the Indian Nations, who once Inhabited Pennsylvania and the Neighbouring States, *in* Transactions of the American Philosophical Society, *volume 1 (1819), pp. 262-271.*

I believe that no sufficiently detailed account has yet been given of the manner in which the North American Indians conduct the funerals of their dead. Captain Carver tells us that the Naudowessies, among whom he was, kept those ceremonies a secret, and would not give him an opportunity of witnessing them. Loskiel, although he drew his information from the journals of our Missionaries, has treated this subject rather superficially. I therefore run little risk of repetition in describing what I have myself seen, and I hope that the particulars which I am going to relate will not be thought uninteresting.

It is well known that the Indians pay great respect to the memory of the dead, and commit their remains to the ground with becoming ceremonies. Those ceremonies, however, are not the same in all cases, but vary according to circumstances, and the condition of the deceased; for rank and wealth receive distinctions even after death, as well among savages as among civilised nations. This, perhaps, may be easily accounted for. When a great chief dies, his death is considered as a national loss; of course all must join in a public demonstration of their sorrow. The rich man, on the other hand, had many friends during his life, who cannot decently abandon him the moment the breath is out of his body; besides, his fortune supplies the means of a rich entertainment at the funeral, of which many, as may well be supposed, are anxious to partake. Thus social distinctions are found even in the state of nature, where perfect equality, if it exists any where, might with the greatest probability be supposed to be found. Though the earth and its fruits are common to all the Indians, yet every man is permitted to enjoy the earnings of his industry, and that produces riches; and though there is no hereditary or even elective rank in their social organization, yet as power follows courage and talents, those who are generally acknowledged to be possessed of those qualities, assume their station above the rest, and the distinction of rank is thus established. Politicians and philosophers may reason on these facts as they please; the descriptions that I give are from nature, and I leave it to abler men than myself to draw the proper inferences from them.

On the death of a principal chief, the village resounds from one end to the other with the loud lamentations of the women, among whom those who sit by the corpse distinguish themselves by the shrillness of their cries and the frantic expression of their sorrow. This scene of mourning over the dead body continues by day and by night until it is interred, the mourners being relieved from time to time by other women.

These honours of "mourning over the corpse" are paid to all; the poor and humble, as well as the rich, great, and powerful; the difference consists only in the number of mourners, the undistinguished Indian having a few besides his immediate relations and friends, and sometimes only those. Women, (notwithstanding all that has been said of their supposed inferior station and of their being reduced to the rank of slaves) are not treated after their death with less respect than the men, and the greatest honours are paid to the remains of the wives of renowned warriors or veteran chiefs, particularly if they were descended themselves of a high family, which, however strange it may appear, is not an indifferent thing among the Indians, who love to honour the merit of their great men in their relatives. I was present in the year 1762, at the funeral of a woman of the highest rank and respectability, the wife of the valiant Delaware chief *Shingask*; as all the honours were paid to her at her interment that are usual on such occasions, I trust a particular description of the ceremony will not be unacceptable.

At the moment that she died, her death was announced through the village by women specially appointed for that purpose, who went through the streets crying, *"She is no more! she is no more!"* The place on a sudden exhibited a scene of universal mourning; cries and lamentations were heard from all quarters; it was truly the expression of the general feeling for a general loss.

The day passed in this manner amidst sorrow and desolation. The next morning, between nine and ten o'clock, two counsellors came to announce to Mr. Thomas Calhoon, the Indian trader, and myself, that we were desired to attend and assist at the funeral which was soon to take place. We, in consequence, proceeded to the house of the deceased, where we found her corpse lying in a coffin, (which had been made by Mr. Calhoon's carpenter) dressed and painted in the most superb Indian style. Her garments, all new, were set off with rows of silver broaches, one row joining the other. Over the sleeves of her new ruffled shirt were broad silver arm spangles from her shoulder down to her wrist, on which were bands, forming a kind of mittens, worked together of wampum, in the same manner as the belts which they use when they deliver speeches. Her long plaited hair was confined by broad bands of silver, one band joining the other, yet not of the same size, but tapering from the head downwards and running at the lower end to a point. On the neck were hanging five broad belts of wampum tied together at the ends, each of a size smaller than the other, the largest of which reached below her breast, the next largest reaching to a few inches of it, and so on, the uppermost one being the smallest. Her scarlet leggings were decorated with different coloured ribands sewed on, the outer edges being finished off with small beads also of various colours. Her mocksens were ornamented with the most striking figures, wrought on the leather with coloured porcupine quills, on the borders of which, round the ancles, were fastened a number of small round silver bells, of about the size of a musket ball. All these things, together with the vermilion paint, judiciously laid on, so as to set her off in the highest style, decorated her person in such a manner, that perhaps nothing of the kind could exceed it.

The spectators having retired, a number of articles were brought out of the house and placed in the coffin, wherever there was room to put them in, among which were a new shirt, a dressed deer skin for shoes, a pair of scissors, needles, thread, a knife, pewter basin and spoon, pint cup, and other similar things, with a number of trinkets and other small articles which she was fond of while living. The lid was then fastened on the coffin with three straps, and three handsome round poles, five or six feet long, were laid across it, near each other, and one in the middle, which were also fastened with straps cut up from a tanned elk hide; and a small bag of vermilion paint, with some flannel to lay it on, was then thrust into the coffin through the hole cut out at the head of it. This hole, the Indians say, is for the spirit of the deceased to go in and out at pleasure, until it has found the place of its future residence.

Every thing being in order, the bearers of the corpse were desired to take their places. Mr. Calhoon and myself were placed at the foremost pole, two women at the middle and two men at the pole in the rear. Several women from a house about thirty yards off, now started off, carrying large kettles, dishes, spoons, and dried elk meat in baskets, for the burial place, and the signal being given for us to move with the body, the women who acted as chief mourners made the air resound with their shrill cries. The order of the procession was as follows: first a leader or guide, from the spot where we were to the place of interment. Next followed the corpse, and close to it *Shingask*, the husband of the deceased. He was followed by the principal war chiefs and counsellors of the nation, after whom came men of all ranks and descriptions. Then followed the women and children, and lastly two stout men carrying loads of European manufactured goods upon their backs. The chief mourners on the women's side, not having joined in the ranks, took their own course to the right, at the distance of about fifteen or twenty yards from us, but always opposite to the corpse. As the corpse had to be carried by the strength of our arms to the distance of about two hundred yards, and hung low between the bearers, we had to rest several times by the way, and whenever we stopped, every body halted until we moved on again.

Being arrived at the grave, we were told to halt, then the lid of the coffin was again taken off, and the body exposed to view. Now the whole train formed themselves into a kind of semi-lunar circle on the south side of the grave, and seated themselves on the ground. Within this circle, at the distance of about fifteen yards from the grave, a common seat was made for Mr. Calhoon and myself to sit on, while the disconsolate *Shingask* retired by himself to a spot at some distance, where he was seen weeping, with his head bowed to the ground. The female mourners seated themselves promiscuously near to each other, among some low bushes that were at the distance of from twelve to fifteen yards east of the grave.

In this situation we remained for the space of more than two hours; not a sound was heard from any quarter, though the numbers that attended were very great; nor did any person move from his seat to view the body, which had been lightly covered over with a clean white sheet. All appeared to be in profound reflection and solemn mourning. Sighs and sobs were now and then heard from the female mourners, so uttered as not to disturb the assembly; it seemed rather as if intended to keep the feeling of sorrow alive in a manner becoming the occasion. Such was the impression made on us by this long silence.

At length, at about one o'clock in the afternoon, six men stepped forward to put the lid upon the coffin, and let down the body into the grave, when suddenly three of the women mourners rushed from their seats, and forcing themselves between these men and the corpse, loudly called out to the deceased to "arise and go with them and not to forsake them." They even took hold of her arms and legs; at first it seemed as if they were caressing her, afterwards they appeared to pull with more violence, as if they intended to run away with the body, crying out all the while, "Arise, arise! Come with us! Don't leave us! Don't abandon us!" At last they retired, plucking at their garments, pulling their hair, and uttering loud cries and lamentations, with all the appearance of frantic despair. After they were seated on the ground, they continued in the same manner crying and sobbing and pulling at the grass and shrubs, as if their minds were totally bewildered and they did not know what they were doing.

As soon as these women had gone through their part of the ceremony, which took up about fifteen minutes, the six men whom they had interrupted and who had remained at the distance of about five feet from the corpse, again stepped forward and did their duty. They let down the coffin into the earth, and laid two thin poles of about four inches diameter, from which the bark had been taken off, lengthways and close together over the grave, after which they retired: Then the husband of the deceased advanced with a very slow pace, and when he came to the grave, walked over it on these poles, and proceeded forward in the same manner into an extensive adjoining prairie, which commenced at this spot.

When the widowed chief had advanced so far that he could not hear what was doing at the grave, a painted post, on which were drawn various figures, emblematic of the deceased's situation in life and of her having been the wife of a valiant warrior, was brought by two men and delivered to a third, a man of note, who placed it in such a manner that it rested on the coffin at the head of the grave, and took great care that a certain part of the drawings should be exposed to the East, or rising of the sun; then, while he held the post erect and properly situated, some women filled up the grave with hoes, and having placed dry leaves and pieces of bark over it, so that none of the fresh ground was visible, they retired, and some men, with timbers fitted before hand for the purpose, enclosed the grave about breast-high, so as to secure it from the approach of the wild beasts.

The whole work being finished, which took up about an hour's time, Mr. Calhoon and myself expected that we might be permitted to go home, as we wished to do, particularly as we saw a thundergust from the west fast approaching; but the Indians, suspecting our design, soon came forward with poles and blankets, and in a few minutes erected a shelter for us.

The storm, though of short duration, was tremendous; the water, produced by the rain, flowing in streams; yet all had found means to secure themselves during its continuance, and being on prairie ground, we were out of all danger of trees being torn up or blown down upon us. Our encampment now appeared like a village, or rather like a military camp, such was the number of places of shelter that had been erected.

Fortunately, the husband of the deceased had reached the camp in good time, and now the gust being over, every one was served with victuals that had been cooked at some distance from the spot. After the repast was over, the articles of merchandise which had been brought by the two men in the rear, having been made up in parcels, were distributed among all present. No one from the oldest to the youngest, was excepted, and every one partook of the liberal donation. This difference only was made, that those who had rendered the greatest services received the most valuable presents, and we were much pleased to see the female mourners well rewarded, as they had, indeed, a very hard task to perform. Articles of little value, such as gartering, tape, needles, beads, and the like, were given to the smaller girls; the older ones received a pair of scissars, needles and thread, and a yard or two of riband. The boys had a knife, jews-harp, awl-blades, or something of similar value. Some of the grown persons received a new suit of clothes, consisting of a blanket, shirt, breech-cloth and leggings, of the value in the whole of about eight dollars; and the women, (I mean those who had rendered essential services) a blanket, ruffled shirts, stroud and leggings, the whole worth from ten to twelve dollars. Mr. Calhoon and myself were each presented with a silk cravat and a pair of leggings. The goods distributed on this occasion, were estimated by Mr. Calhoon at two hundred dollars; the greatest part of them had, the same morning, been taken out of his store.

After we had thus remained, in a manner, under confinement, for more than six hours, the procession ended, and Mr. Calhoon and myself retired with the rest to our homes. At dusk a kettle of victuals was carried to the grave and placed upon it, and the same was done every evening for the space of three weeks, at the end of which it was supposed that the traveller had found her place of residence. During that time the lamentations of the women-mourners were heard on the evenings of each day, though not so loud nor so violent as before.

I have thus described, from minutes which I took at the time, the ceremonies which take place among the Delaware Indians on the death of a person of high rank and consideration among them. The funerals of persons of an inferior station are conducted with less pomp and with less expense. When the heirs of the deceased cannot afford to hire female mourners, the duty is performed by their own immediate relations and friends. But "mourning over the corpse," is a ceremony that cannot be dispensed with.

It is always customary, when an Indian dies, of whatever rank or condition he may be, to put a number of the articles which belonged to the deceased in the coffin or grave, that he may have them when wanted. I have seen a bottle of rum or whiskey placed at the coffin head, and the reason given for it was, that the deceased was fond of liquor while living, and he would be glad of a dram when he should feel fatigued on his journey to the world of spirits.

When an Indian dies at a distance from his home, great care is taken that the grave be well fortified with posts and logs laid upon it, that the wolves may be prevented from getting at the corpse; when time and circumstances do not permit this, as, for instance, when the Indians are travelling, the body is enclosed in the bark of trees and thus laid in the grave. When a death takes place at their hunting camps, they make a kind of coffin as well as they can, or put a cover over the body, so that the earth may not sink on it, and then enclose the grave with a fence of poles.

Warriors that are slain in battle, are, if possible, drawn aside and buried, so that the enemy may not get their scalps, and also that he may not know the number of the slain. In such cases, they will turn an old log out of its bed, and dig a grave so deep, that the log, when replaced, may not press too hard upon the body. If any of the fresh earth be seen, they cover it with rotten wood, brush or leaves, that its place may not be found. If they have not sufficient time for this, or the number of their dead is too great, they throw the bodies on the top of each other between large logs, and place any kind of rotten wood or other rubbish upon them. They never, when they can help it, leave their dead to be devoured by wild beasts.

When the Indians have to speak of a deceased person, they never mention him or her by name, lest they should renew the grief of the family or friends. They say, "He who was our counsellor or chief," "She who was the wife of our friend;" or they will allude to some particular circumstance, as that of the deceased having been with them at a particular time or place, or having done some particular act or spoken particular words which they all remember, so that every body knows who is meant. I have often observed with emotion this remarkable delicacy, which certainly does honour to their hearts, and shews that they are naturally accessible to the tenderest feelings of humanity.

VIII. EPILOGUE

Thomas Morton, an English lawyer and gentleman, came to Massachusetts about 1623 where he proceeded to earn the enmity of the Plymouth Pilgrims 25 miles to the south by trading guns and liquor to the Indians, coaxing indentured servants away from their masters, and erecting a maypole at "Merrymount". In 1637 he published a defense of his free-spirited life-style entitled New English Canaan, *a reprint of which was issued by Peter Force in 1838 in his* Tracts and other Papers, relating principally to the Origin, Settlement, and Progress of the Colonies in North America *(Washington). The following passage appears on pp. 38-40 of that edition.*

A gentleman and a traveller, that had bin in the parts of New England for a time, when hee retorned againe in his discourse of the Country, wondered (as hee said,) that the natives of the land lived so poorely, in so rich a Country, like to our Beggers in England: Surely that Gentleman had not time or leasure whiles hee was there, truely to informe himselfe of the state of that Country, and the happy life the Salvages would leade weare they once brought to Christianity.

I must confesse they want the use and benefit of Navigation (which is the very sinnus of a flourishing Commonwealth,) yet are they supplied with all manner of needfull things, for the maintenance of life and lifelyhood, Foode and rayment are the cheife of all that we make true use of; and of these they finde no want, but have, them in a most plentifull manner.

If our beggers of England should with so much ease (as they,) furnish themselves with foode, at all seasons, there would not be so many starved in the streets, neither would so many gaoles be stuffed, or gallouses furnished with poore wretches, as I have seene them.

But they of this sort of our owne nation, that are fitt to goe to this Canaan are not able to transport themselves, and most of them unwilling to goe from the good ale tap; which is the very loadstone of the lande by which our English beggers steere theire Course: it is the Northpole to which the flowre-deluce of their compasse points; the more is the pitty that the Commonalty of oure Land are of such leaden capacities, as to neglect so brave a Country, that doth so plentifully feede Maine lusty and a brave, able men, women, and children that have not the meanes that a Civilized Nation hath to purchase foode and rayment: which that Country with a little industry will yeeld a man in a very comfortable measure; without overmuch carking.

I cannot deny but a civilized Nation, hath the preheminence of an uncivilized, by meanes of those instruments that are found to be common amongst civile people, and the uncivile want the use of, to make themselves masters of those ornaments, that make such a glorious shew, that will give a man occasion to cry, *sic transit gloria Mundi*.

Now since it is but foode and rayment that men that live needeth (though not all alike,) why should not the Natives of New England be sayd to live richly having no want of either: Cloaths are the badge of sinne, and the more variety of fashions is but the greater abuse of the Creature, the beasts of the forrest there doe serve to furnish them at any time, when they please: fish and flesh they have in greate abundance which they both roast and boyle.

They are indeed not served in dishes of plate with variety of Sauces to procure appetite, that needs not there. The rarity of the aire begot by the medicinable quality of the sweete herbes of the Country, alwayes procures good stomakes to the inhabitants.

I must needs commend them in this particular, that though they buy many commodities of our Nation, yet they keepe but fewe, and those of speciall use.

They love not to bee cumbered with many utensilles, and although every proprietor knowes his owne, yet all things (so long as they will last,) are used in common amongst them: A bisket cake given to one; that one breakes it equally into so many parts, as there be persons in his company, and distributes it. Platoes Commonwealth is so much practised by these people.

According to humane reason guided onely by the light of nature, these people leades the more happy and freer life, being voyde of care, which torments the mindes of so many Christians: They are not delighted in baubles, but in usefull things.

Their naturall drinke is of the Christall fountaine, and this they take up in their hands, by joyning them close together. They take up a great quantity at a time, and drinke at the wrists. It was the sight of such a feate, which made Diogenes hurle away his dishe, and like one that would have this principall confirmed. *Natura paucis contentat*, used a dish no more.

I have observed that they will not be troubled with superfluous commodities. Such things as they finde, they are taught by necessity to make use of they will make choise of; and seeke to purchase with industry so that in respect, that their life is so voyd of care, and they are so loving also that they make use of those things they enjoy (the wife onely excepted) as common goods, and are therein, so compassionate that rather than one should starve through want, they would starve all, thus doe they passe away the time merrily, not regarding our pompe (which they see dayly before their faces) but are better content with their owne, which some men esteeme so meanely of.

They may be rather accompted to live richly wanting nothing that is needefull; and to be commended for leading a contented life, the younger being ruled by the Elder, and the Elder ruled by the Powahs, and the Powahs are ruled by the Devill, and then you may imagin what good rule is like to be amongst them.